# WHO CARES

FLEMING H. REVELL COMPANY
WESTWOOD • NEW JERSEY

WHO

# A. Reuben Gornitzka

# CARES

*To three blondes and a brunette—four
daughters, Lynn, Kassy, Nikka, and Phoebe—
who alternately spoiled or pleasantly
harassed the lone male in the household.*

# PREFACE

"I couldn't care less!" It's been said innumerable times by so many. Sometimes we say it seriously about a serious something; sometimes only jokingly about the unimportant. But we do say it often, seriously, and, much more tragically, about *somebody*, not just something.

Who cares—*really* cares—both about important things and about people, all of whom are important? Who cares? Many would cynically reply, "Nobody." At least to them this would be the answer. Whether it be the fault of others, or their own fault, or a combination of both, this would be their answer to either the terse or the flippant question, "Who cares?"

"Yes," you say; but if you do care very much about very many people, you can get not so nicely "burned." You are right—you can and very surely will, on occasion, be hurt. There *is* risk involved. But not very much in life of any worth is without the element of risk. Even the birth of mankind involved that. And one can go on and on, from way back then to here and now, where we find ourselves seriously asking the questions: "Who cares?" "Why?" "About what and whom?" We are tempted to say, "I couldn't care less," but just possibly we can discover some secrets which would lead us to say, "I couldn't care more."

# CONTENTS

# 1. Who Wants to Get Involved!

A truck loaded with cans of beer had some trouble rounding a sharp bend along a Connecticut highway and overturned, spilling its cargo all over the road. The traffic was fairly heavy at the time, and lots of cars sped past, but nobody stopped to see whether the truck driver had been hurt. Fortunately, he was only shaken up a bit and was able to pull himself out of the wrecked truck.

He took one look at the beer cans rolling along the road and realized what a traffic hazard they were. So he walked down the highway until he came to one of those lonely little telephone booths and called the police to report the accident. Then he called a mechanic, told him where his truck was, and walked back to the scene of the accident. In that short amount of time, every single can of beer had vanished! When the police arrived, the truck driver even had a hard time convincing them that there ever had been any cargo at all in his truck— until they began to spot empty beer cans farther down the road where people had thrown them from their cars.

Nobody wanted to stop and offer a helping hand to a truck driver—but they didn't mind pulling over to the side of the road to pick up a can of beer. It kind of shakes our faith in human nature, doesn't it?

Where is everybody these days? Where were they when a young woman named Kitty Genovese came home from work late one night and was attacked by a man with a knife? She was right in front of her apartment house

11

on a street in New York City, and she was completely visible in the light from street lamps. And where was everybody? Oh, people were there, all right—thirty-eight of Kitty Genovese's neighbors heard her pitiful screams and ran to their windows to find out what was going on. But something happened to those people, and we may never learn what it was. Not a single one of them made a move to help the bleeding girl on the sidewalk. Not a single one of them answered her when she looked up and pleaded, "Help me, for God's sake!" No one even called the police.

Oh, yes, a few of those people called out to the attacker —"Hey, leave her alone!"—and at first the man drew back into the shadows. Then, when no one came to help the girl, the man came back to stalk her as she tried to drag herself to the shelter of a doorway. For thirty minutes he followed her, inch by inch, stabbing her repeatedly, and all that time under the eyes of thirty-eight witnesses. Finally, the job was done and the attacker left —Kitty Genovese was dead. Then somebody got up enough nerve to call the police and report the crime.

Have you ever heard a noise in the night—the screech of brakes, or the shriek of a merrymaker—and rushed to your window, half-dreading what you might see? It happens often, and we're usually relieved to find absolutely nothing out there in the darkness. But someday— or some night—we might see something—or someone— that needs our help, and we'd like to think we'd be ready to give it, wouldn't we? But we can't be sure. If Kitty Genovese had had only one neighbor, the story might not be so shocking. One person might easily become paralyzed with fear. But—thirty-eight?

We may try to comfort ourselves with the thought that such things happen in New York, but not anywhere else.

I wonder—and someone else wondered, too. A young reporter in San Bernardino, California, read about Kitty Genovese and shook his head over the behavior of "some people." Then he got to thinking—were the people of San Bernardino any different? He talked to his editor about it, and they decided to put their community to a test. They "planted" a seedy, shabbily dressed man in the gutter of a main street, and they stood back to wait, watch, and photograph. They saw people pass by, and some of them stopped—but not for very long. Those who stopped turned away in disgust, probably assuming the man was drunk, and many others simply stared as they continued to walk by. No one tried to help the man —no one even wanted to find out whether he were alive or dead. The next day, the story and photographs appeared on the front page of a San Bernardino newspaper, and proved that people in that city couldn't look down their moral noses at the people in New York City. And neither can we.

Some distressing things are happening lately, and some of us are getting to the point where we don't even want to pick up a newspaper any more. We might read about the young man who took his fiancée swimming in Fairbanks, Alaska, recently, and never lived to marry her. The girl was on shore when the boy went in the water for a last swim, and then it happened. He got a severe cramp and shouted for help before he sank beneath the surface. There were other swimmers near him, but no one made a move to help him. His fiancée saw him go under and rushed into the water—but by the time she reached the spot where he had gone down, there wasn't a trace of him, not even a bubble on the water. I wonder how she felt about those other swimmers who might have saved his life.

There's a man in Dallas, Texas, today who is still alive, although a number of people did their best—or their worst—to take his life. First he was robbed; then he was shot three times by his assailants and dumped from their speeding car onto the road. Somehow he managed to get to his feet and he staggered along the side of the road, trying to flag down one of the passing cars. Yes, he was covered with blood, and I suppose he must have frightened some people, because a lot of cars passed him by. Then, one driver evidently felt more compassion than fear and he stopped to pick up the desperate man. He saved his life by getting him to a hospital in time.

Children used to be able to melt the hardest hearts, but not any more. Nobody lifted a hand to help a little three-year-old girl who was bitten by a stray dog in Los Angeles' Union Station. They just formed a circle and stared while the child's mother begged them to find a doctor, or try to catch the dog—or something, anything!

I guess old people understand loneliness better than anyone else because their advanced age often takes them beyond the life span of their friends and even their relatives. It's terrible to live a lonely life, but one of the saddest stories I've ever read concerned a lonely death. It seems that a 73-year-old woman who had lived alone in her home for many years died—and her body wasn't discovered until fourteen days later! Now, that means that no one even cared enough to knock on her door, to telephone her, to write her a letter—even the merchants who had delivered her food for many years didn't ask what had become of her. It makes you wonder whether anyone cared about that poor old woman during any of those seventy-three years.

I guess we've all heard and read and lived too many of these stories lately, and we're beginning to feel pretty disturbed by them—disturbed enough, perhaps, to ask ourselves some questions. What's happening to people today? Don't they care about each other any more? What about our neighbors? Would they give us a helping hand if we were in trouble? And even more important—would we go to their aid? Maybe that's the biggest question of all, maybe that's the core of the problem. Do we care? Do we want to get involved?

## 2. Whatever Happened to Adam?

Some people seem to be able to live in isolation, at least for a little while. Not long ago some scientists were conducting an important experiment in France and they used a remarkable type of guinea pig. They wanted to determine the effects of complete isolation on the mind, body, and spirit of a human being so that they could learn what to expect from people who would someday make the long journey to the moon. Their guinea pig was a young Frenchwoman who volunteered to spend eighty-eight days alone down in a cave. She was to have all the comforts of home—except companionship and a means of communication. She wasn't even allowed to take along a watch or any other timepiece.

After eighty-eight days the young woman returned to the surface of the earth, apparently in very good condition. She had lost track of time and thought it was two weeks earlier than it really was, but she seemed to suffer no other ill effects from her solitary confinement. She had kept busy, she said, by knitting, reading some books, and daydreaming.

That's the way some people are, and they don't always have to go down in a cave to get away from the world. Some people carry a cave around with them. I'll never forget a man I saw when I was walking through a hotel lobby one rainy day. He passed by with his head bent as far down as it would go, and I was absolutely fascinated by the skill with which he avoided bumping into people.

All he could see was their shoes, but apparently that was enough. In fact, it occurred to me at that moment that he was probably an authority on shoes—and on lost coins, puddles, dusty scraps of paper, and cracks in the sidewalk. But I don't think he knew much about people from the ankles on up. I often wonder about that man—was he afraid to look up?

Lots of people are afraid—that feeling goes back to the very first man on earth. If you glance through history, you'll find him hiding in the bushes and covering his ears with his hands because he didn't want to hear God calling his name. "Adam—where are you?" God called, but Adam didn't want to come out into the open.

And shortly after, God looked down on one of Adam's sons and called, "Cain—where is your brother?"

God is still asking these two questions, and so are most of us, even if we don't say the words aloud. Where are all the Adams hiding these days while so many terrible things are happening to the rest of us? Doesn't anybody give a hoot about the Abels any more?

Suppose we need help?—will the Adams come running? Or are they hiding in the bushes with their hands over their ears? Are they rubbing their fists in their eyes so they won't see Cain clubbing down Abel?

But there aren't any bushes left in this small, televised world of ours, so where can the Adams be hiding? There are so many people on earth today, so many houses packed close together, and TV and radio have made the world's acoustics so sensitive that every cry of pain can be heard all around the world in a matter of seconds.

No, Adam can't hide in the bushes these days, but he's hiding out, just the same. He walks the streets with the rest of us; he lives in the same building, or maybe down the street; he breaks his neck to catch the same train home at night; and he may even be squinting back at us from the mirror in the hallway. Adam is everywhere—but try to find him when you need him!

Adam has a new gimmick today. He can be right in the middle of things and still not be part of them. You see, he has a new hideout, a sort of invisible cave. It's called, "I Don't Want to Get Involved," a handy little device that cuts him off from people. He doesn't even have to cover his eyes; he sees everything that's going on, yet nothing gets through to him.

Does this Adam look too familiar to us? Do we recognize something of ourselves in him, and does it make us feel uncomfortable? Can it really be true that we don't care what happens to the rest of the human race? That certainly wasn't the philosophy that got this country started on its magnificent course in the world, but things have a way of changing, and not always for the better. Maybe we're going through a stage. Maybe we've gone through the stages of loving God, and then reason, and then science—and perhaps now we love only ourselves!

If that's true, then our situation is like the cartoon of the shipwrecked man who stands looking at a note he found in a bottle washed up on his desert island—and the note reads, "I am sorry I cannot be of any help to you. I do not want to get involved!"

But we're not shipwrecked—at least, not yet. And we're not on a lonely island. We're in God's world of people. Whoever we are and whatever we do have an effect on that world, and if we turn our backs on people it's going to do something to them. Have you taken a good look at the world lately—even from a distance?

## 3.   A Case of Contagion

Recently I had an opportunity to ride in a helicopter over a short stretch of the California landscape, and it was a beautiful experience. There we were, cruising along in the air, now and then stopping, hovering—almost motionless, like some giant insect—over a particularly breathtaking bit of scenery. All of a sudden I turned my head to look out of a window on the other side of the cockpit and saw what I thought must be the finest golf course in the world. I hadn't ever heard of a golf course in that area, but the land was so green, so perfectly terraced, that it couldn't be anything else. Then I looked again, more carefully this time, and I discovered what it really was—a cemetery.

And then the characteristics of the land beneath the helicopter began to change. We were passing over the freeways, those frantic veins of a large metropolitan area, so choked with life and convulsed with death, and I glanced backward again toward the cemetery. Those two landmarks may have seemed different at first, but they had something in common. Those expressways—built for business and recreational purposes—were becoming one big cemetery for Americans on wheels. There are 70 million automobiles on our roads today, and last year there were 47,800 highway fatalities, and the number is expected to grow every year unless someone comes up with a way to stop this mass murder.

This is the kind of thing that happens when people stop

caring about people—when one driver doesn't want to get involved in another person's safety. I think most of us have a fairly healthy regard for the value of our own skins, but apparently that isn't enough.

You can learn a lot out there on the highway. You'll find all kinds of reading matter as you drive along—all sorts of posters telling you not to throw your trash out on the road, not to throw lighted cigarettes or matches out the car window. You may even think that some of the warnings are exaggerated until you pass the charred remains of a once-vigorous forest. You'd be amazed at the devastation one careless person can cause because he didn't want to get involved in the preservation of trees, wildlife, and some of nature's most generous gifts.

Haven't you noticed? Some people are conducting campaigns to wake us up to our carelessness! We're beginning to run out of our resources in this great land of ours, but we still aren't doing much to stop the waste and abuse of our heritage. We're running short of water in some parts of the country, and the air we breathe is becoming more and more polluted every day. If you enjoy eating fish, you've probably noticed that there's a shortage of lobsters and oysters in restaurants. What's going to be next? Or doesn't anyone care?

As life becomes more automated, we're supposed to have more leisure time. What are we going to do with it? If you can make your way through the heavy traffic out of the cities and into the countryside, where will you go? The old swimming hole is dried up, and the old fishing pond is slick with industrial waste. The trees have been cut down, or burned down, and you can't find a bit of shade anywhere. Everything has been used up—what a shame!

Cities have shortages, too. They're running out of space,

horizontally and vertically, and now they're beginning to tear down old buildings so that they can make room for new ones. This is great for architects and contractors, but kind of hard on the people who have to get out of the way. How do you suppose people feel when they have to pull up stakes to make room for an office building? Or doesn't anyone want to suppose?

New York City is soon going to have a new expressway—and some very unhappy citizens whose homes have been disrupted by it. First, these people had to move out of the way of the new road, and most of them found apartments a few blocks away so that they could stay in their old neighborhood. Now the city wants to build a housing project for all the families who were forced to move—and those unfortunate people have to move again to make way for the new apartments which they don't want. Can you blame these people for feeling that nobody cares what happens to them?

We may not mean to hurt anyone when we turn our backs on the world and think only of ourselves, but we do some damage just the same. For one thing, we set a bad example. Somebody watches us shrug our shoulders and turn away, and he thinks, "Why should *I* bother?" And so it goes, until carelessness and unconcern become diseases with epidemic proportions.

I've had nothing but wonderful experiences with PTA groups—and I've spoken to a great many of them. I've found them to be interested, alert, and concerned people; but evidently I haven't met the other kind, the kind who couldn't care less about what happens in their communities.

Some of our newspapers report that many PTA's are in trouble because their members are apathetic. In a town in West Virginia, for example, the 45-year-old PTA was

21

disbanded last year because so few members attended the meetings; and those who came didn't seem to care enough to ask questions, make decisions, and form policies. That's epidemic-sized carelessness, isn't it? I wonder how the teachers in that town feel about the lack of interest in the school system—or maybe they don't care, either!

Could this happen in your town, to your PTA? Can you do anything to stop it? Apathy is like a virus, once it gets going in a town or a nation. You can almost see it strike down one victim after another, and before long you may find yourself coming down with a touch of it. Watch out —it may turn into something serious!

## 4. The Morals Gap

I don't know much about chemistry, and even less about physics and electronics, but I hold my breath in amazement every time a satellite goes up to orbit this earth. I don't suppose I'm very different from everyone else these days—we're all impressed with the fantastic scientific achievements being made almost every day. It's an exciting time to be alive!

Not so long ago, people would have thought that one discovery per generation was quite a record, but we live in a different world today. We've come to expect discoveries and we're seldom disappointed. Who would have believed that within a few years' time we would have such things as penicillin, vaccine against polio—pill or innoculation, take your pick!—a Laser ray, a Telstar, and all kinds of machines to work and even think for us! This is an age of progress!

But a funny thing is happening on our way to the moon. We're going places fast with our bodies—but our souls are falling behind. As a nation we have a wonderful capacity to leap ahead scientifically, while at the same time there seems to be a peculiar lag in our ethics, our morals, our spiritual welfare. This is a warning that used to come from the pulpits, and hardly anywhere else—but it comes from a lot of other sources today. Just turn on your radio, or open your newspaper, or get together with your neighbors.

Ask some people who work in department stores—

they'll tell you what's happening to our ethical standards. "Thou shalt not steal" is a joke to many people today— and very few of them are poor. As our large stores provide more and more self-service features to help turn the wheels of commerce a little faster, they're finding out that it isn't so profitable after all. They may save money by cutting down on their sales help, but they're losing a small fortune to shoplifters—who, incidentally, still do everything by hand! And do you know who most of these small-time thieves turn out to be? Kids! Most of them are kids out for kicks. Shoplifting has become sort of a game for them.

Embezzlement is costing businessmen much of their profits, and I'm not talking about embezzlement of large amounts of money. It's the little embezzlements that are breaking the back of industry today—the thousands and thousands of paper clips, rubber bands, sheets of paper, envelopes, pads, pencils, gummed tape, staples, and stamps, oh, the stamps!

Do you still have all the hubcaps on your car? You're lucky—most people have lost one or two. They're easy to steal, and some kids have developed a skill of removing one in a matter of seconds. These kids aren't always hungry, either—some of them don't even peddle the hubcaps they steal. They just bend them and throw them away—all the fun was in the stealing!

Is your son or daughter ready to go to college? Are you a little nervous about it, afraid they might run into this "new morality" that is supposed to be brazenly taking over the campuses in America? We hear some hair-raising stories about life on campus, and we know that much of it is nothing more than exaggeration for the sake of selling newspapers and magazines. But some of it must be the truth, and that's enough to make any parent worry.

According to some reports, our children don't care about such things as morals or principles any more—they don't seem to care about anything at all.

Most of us are ashamed of some of the things that are happening in our country lately, and we don't like the rest of the world to see them, either. We get a little touchy when a foreign country shakes its head over some of our riots, our murders, our violence in the streets, and we wonder why people don't turn their attention to the wonderful features of our country. And yet, we can't help but realize that there are shadows and clouds around us, darkening the bright hope that once was our most prominent American feature. Other countries aren't really picking on us, are they? They're simply pointing a finger at the contrast between what we say and what we do. They want to know whether we really mean what we say—and we wonder, too, perhaps.

What's wrong with us? we ask ourselves. How could our whole moral fiber become so weakened that it shows up as some kind of spiritual scurvy in our young people? Where does the blame belong? When did it all begin to happen? Could we have done something about it a long time ago so that we wouldn't have to live with disgrace now? That's one of the problems, isn't it? We don't quite remember how it all started because we were busy with our own private lives then. We were minding our own business, then. Maybe we didn't want to get involved.

## 5. Will Your Parachute Open?

One spring a few years ago I was one of several people invited by the Secretary of the Navy to be his guests at Pensacola, Florida, for three days. It was a fascinating and an eventful visit, and the Navy put on a spectacular show for us.

We saw lightening-swift jet aircraft; we saw the latest fire-fighting equipment; and we even spent a day on an aircraft carrier, watching the takeoffs and landings. To add to the excitement, we were privileged to observe preparations for a very special event: an attempt to set a new record in the ascent of a Navy balloon.

I had a chance to talk to the two men who were to go up in the balloon, and that made me await the event with even greater interest. They were fine young men, and I caught some of their eagerness to push on into the unknown.

The balloon went up and everything went well, and it seemed that there might be no need for the helicopters, which would ordinarily handle the after-flight pickup. The weather was clear—absolutely perfect for such a test—and only one thing remained to be done before the flight was finished. The balloon, as it descended, was to attempt an unusual landing on the aircraft carrier, a somewhat difficult maneuver.

The world's record for balloon ascension had been broken, and down came the balloon, just missing the carrier. It landed in the water, and immediately the helicopters closed in on the spot. Slings were lowered from the 'copters to the men in the water, and everyone gave a sigh of relief. One man was pulled into a 'copter—and suddenly the other man slipped out of his sling and down into the water twenty-five feet below! His clothing pulled him under quickly, and before anyone could reach him he drowned.

I don't think I'll ever forget that tragic event, not only because I had met the young man, but because there was a kind of lesson in it. It seemed to say that we human beings can climb up to the loftiest intellectual and scientific mountain peaks—only to fall off other of life's cliffs when we least expect it. And what happens to us then? Naturally we can't hope to go through our lives without falling off a cliff now and then—but how do we keep from breaking to bits on the rocks below? I suppose most of us assume that we carry some sort of spiritual parachutes for those awful moments—but can we be sure those parachutes will open when we pull the cord?

Faith is the parachute we're counting on, but maybe we'd better check the condition of our faith before we go any higher up the mountain. If we haven't been using it lately, it might be full of tiny holes.

How much attention have you been giving to your faith during the past few years? How excited can you get over the meaning of faith in your life? Does it affect your relationship to your job, to society, to your family?—or is it confined to some dingy corner of your life and used only for an hour on Sundays? Some people are finding that their faith, like their moral fiber, has been weakened by neglect—and they're finding out too late.

It's a funny thing, but people who are strong in faith have very little faith in themselves. They know that they have to depend upon other people—and especially upon

God. I remember reading about a spritely Englishwoman who took her first plane ride on her one-hundredth birthday, and loved every minute of it. Yet I know many people who are terrified by the thought of flying, and statistics reveal that many share this fear. It seems that about 80 percent of the flying done in America is done by about 20 percent of the population. In other words, more people aren't flying—the same people are flying more often. Yet even cost has little to do with it any more.

Naturally, many of these people are businessmen who have more opportunity and reason to travel by plane. Still, fear is the most obvious reason why about 38 percent of the people in our country have never been in a plane—*some people are afraid to fly*, even though statistics prove commercial flying to be considerably safer than driving in a car.

How about the rest of us and those ridiculous fears that keep popping up between us and other people? Can we really get along by ourselves? Or will we have to begin trusting somebody, somewhere, someday?

It's nice to have faith in ourselves, but that just isn't enough. It isn't the kind of faith that can hold us up when we're falling, when we need a good, strong parachute. We need a different kind of faith, a tougher kind of faith, the kind that comes from depending on Someone Else— and that kind is going out of style these days.

## 6. The Top—at Any Cost

Don't get me wrong—I'm not opposed to progress, and in fact I'm all for it. I just like to be sure that when I take a step ahead I'm going to put my foot down on firm ground.

Some people who are aiming for the top are climbing a ladder made of air, and I hate to think what will happen when they reach the highest rung. They follow a philosophy I call the "success cult," and any businessman knows what that is. It means that a man is considered a failure if he lands anywhere but on the very top of the business world, and he's not supposed to worry about how he manages to get there. If he has to wear hobnailed boots and climb over the backs of everyone standing in his way, more power to him! Never mind what kind of work he does on his way up to the top, never mind whether he can handle that big job once he gets it—just get it!

If this man starts out with any feelings for other people, he'll soon have to give them up. They don't have any place in his career. Besides, if he doesn't push people aside, they'll jab their elbows in his ribs as they pass him by, won't they? They don't care, so why should he?

This philosophy is the cause of so many of those ulcers you've heard about, and it's sending some very good men off to a miserable future. What are they going to do up there at the top? How will they like the view overlooking a sea of enemies?

There isn't room for everybody at the top, in spite of that old saying, and some people will have to step off somewhere down the line. Maybe they'll even have to get pushed off the ladder, and that's going to hurt.

Fortunately, not all people want to go to the top. Some of them want nothing more than a warm little niche somewhere in the middle where they can curl up in the folds of some nice fringe benefits. Ambition? Not for them! They're too smart to get mixed up in the rat race. They're more interested in the "security cult," which, roughly translated, states that the world owes them a living, and a pretty high-priced one at that. When they apply for a job, they don't ask what the work involves, or what the opportunities are for advancement—they ask how long the hours are, how many coffee breaks there are, how high the salary is, and how soon they can retire?

These are a few signs of our times, but I don't believe that any of us like the direction in which they're pointing. Whatever became of good, old-fashioned pride in our work, in our sense of accomplishment? Practically every job in the world has a fancy title these days, but that will never be able to take the place of a feeling of achievement at the end of the day. When a man does his work well— however humble his job—he can whistle a tune on his way home at night. He can leave his job at the office, or the shop, or the store, and forget about it until the next morning. The fellow who doesn't get involved with his work will never know a feeling of satisfaction. He may have a title, but it doesn't mean anything to him because he's got his eye on another title a little higher up the ladder. He seldom takes his time to learn how to do his job well because he doesn't think success has anything to do with effort. Good workmanship, in his eyes, is an old-fashioned term that doesn't mean anything today because nobody cares about it. This man carries his job around on his back everywhere he goes—he takes it home to his wife and children, he takes it into his dreams and turns some of them into nightmares, and he takes the worst parts of his working day into the dark recesses of his mind, where they start to eat away at him.

How can we say that people don't care about their jobs any more when so many of us seem to think of nothing else? We practically give up our lives for our careers and get very little in return. Let's be sure, though, that we're using the right kind of words when we talk about our jobs. Let's be sure, for instance, that we don't confuse the word "attention" for "care," because they don't mean the same thing. You can give your attention to something without getting wrapped up in it, and isn't this the way some of us think about our daily work? We may be waiting with bated breath for the first sign of the next promotion, or the next salary increase, but are we really involved in our performance?

Unless we can get completely absorbed in our work, to the point where the hours fly, we aren't doing a very good job. Unless we can forget about "What's in it for me?" and look for greater opportunities to be of service to our employers, our communities, our churches, or our fellow-men, then we have no right to expect fantastic guarantees for our future.

The business world is in a peculiar predicament. Everybody wants to be taken care of, but hardly anybody wants to care. This is a strange tug-o'-war that neither side can win. It makes us wonder how it's all going to end, doesn't it?

## 7. "They've Got It Coming!"

People can suffer from too much attention and not enough care at the same time—did you ever realize that? Most of us assume that the rich and famous haven't a worry in the world, but that isn't the way most celebrities look at their lives.

At times we can't help becoming annoyed by the antics of some outstanding people. We sort of expect people of great genius, talent, and ability to set a better example for the rest of us and we're disappointed whenever they exhibit more arrogance than humility.

I know a man like that and I find it very hard to sympathize with his problems—but he certainly has big ones! I know of very few men who have risen to such an important position in the world, and I hope I will never meet another one who is half as cocky. This man does everything well, with one glaring exception—he just can't seem to grasp the meaning of simple graciousness and consideration of others, and this is becoming a tragic flaw in his personality. It may well cost him all his achievements.

When arrogant people fall from great heights, they come down with a loud crash that is usually echoed and described in every detail in newspapers, magazines, and television programs. They can't keep their shame to themselves, and all of us have a chance to shake our heads over them. And a strange thing happens to some of us. We don't always feel sorry for the big shots when they come tumbling down, and sometimes we're just a bit pleased.

Perhaps, without realizing it, we've been envying some famous person for a long time. Maybe we've resented their kind of life, with its abundance of money and power and seeming freedom from the complexities that beset the rest of us. We sometimes think that we're the ones with the *real* problems in life, and we don't like to see some men or women of prominence making a big fuss about "nothing."

This is what happens to people who get too much attention—they get cut off from the rest of the world and they live terribly lonely lives. It's understandable why we should believe that famous people breeze through life without any difficulties, because that is what we're supposed to believe. That's part of being famous. Famous people are supposed to be carefree and perfectly adjusted to our world. You keep your troubles to yourself when you get up there on the top, because, frankly, nobody wants to hear about them. Nobody really cares.

"Who likes me just for me?" a well-known actress asked me one day when we were discussing some of the rather unique problems of her world. "That's my biggest problem," she said, and when I thought about it for a little while I began to understand what she meant. Here was a woman who had worked her way up in a pretty rugged occupational field, and she had faced fierce competition all the way. Oh, she was surrounded by many people— and the crowds grew larger as she got closer to the top— but did they really care what happened to her? Did they shower her with attention because they enjoyed her friendship or wanted to comfort her in the lonely, disillusioned moments when she wondered about the meaning of her life? Or did all those people want to use a talented actress to better themselves? Did they hope to get a break in television or the movies? Did they want her to endorse their products so that they could sell more of them? Did they want to sell her something?

These are questions you and I usually don't have to ask ourselves, and we can be thankful that we don't. We can find out who our friends are without making such painful inquiries—and without finding the more painful answers to them, too.

For all the respect and admiration and attention we give to famous people in the fields of industry, politics, science, entertainment, or the arts, we aren't giving them the concern or the care they—and all of us—really crave. Quite often they were driven to succeed because their lives lacked the love most of us need to keep our personalities in balance, and their disappointment on reaching the top—and finding nothing but the bright, cold spotlight of attention—is very deep.

We're all alike, great and small. As someone once said, we all have to put on one shoe at a time. Each of us, famous or humble, must struggle alone with our problems, with our fears, and each of us needs the security of a great love. The shopkeeper and the statesman have much in common, and so do the mechanic and the industrial magnate: they're all human beings!—tempted, challenged, worried, lonely, and desperately in need of something higher and bigger than their own little egos. The rich and the famous are just like the rest of us.

We human beings are alike in another important respect: we want to be loved—and if not loved, liked—and not for anything we can do, or say, or give away. We want to be liked for ourselves, for the things God gave us as individuals and members of the human race. We don't want to buy love, and we don't want to bribe anyone for it, and we certainly don't want to beg for it—although some of us are reduced to that. *We just want it*—because something in us needs it. I guess that's the only way we can be real persons, and know who we are.

Don't envy people who seem to get a lot of attention—they may not know a single human being who cares whether they live or die. Perhaps the beginning of an answer for them or for anyone is the real discovery of that "first" love, God's. The trouble is that so many can begin to understand that love only by its being reflected by other human beings.

## 8. "Nobody Kisses Me Any More"

A great many little people must feel terribly lonely, terribly cut off from the rest of us, too. At least that's what the alarming number of suicides seem to tell us. Can you imagine life becoming so unbearable that a person would want to snuff it out? That's one of the worst tragedies in our modern world.

We've gone through other times like this, and many of us can remember some of the heart-rending stories that came out of the depression years. I lived in Milwaukee, Wisconsin, following those days, and I remember that the galleries of the county court house had to be screened to prevent people from leaping off the upper stories down to the lobby floor. There are lots of other precautions we can take to keep people from killing themselves, but that doesn't really solve the problem of why they want to do it, does it?

These are disturbing times, and many of us have reason to feel uneasy about something in our lives. Change in itself is frightening, sometimes, especially when things change so rapidly and we have to make sudden adjustments to a whole new way of life. We're all looking for answers to our questions, but some of us have a bit more trouble finding them—and some of us find nothing but despair.

What is it that we all need today? This is the big question, the one the church has been trying to answer in its efforts to help people live in our troubled world.

Many years ago, just after the Japanese attack on Pearl Harbor in 1941, I heard about a young lady who mysteriously left her dormitory on the University of Wisconsin campus late on the evening of the attack. She didn't return to her room for several hours, and when she did, she was of course immediately summoned to the office of the Dean of Women. She was asked to explain her absence, and the distressed girl found it difficult to put her reason into words. Finally, she said that she had gone to pieces when she heard the news report of the bombing attack and simply couldn't remain in her room. So she left and went out into the darkness, not quite knowing where she was heading. Much later, she found herself in front of the capitol building, and she just stood there, staring up at the lighted dome for a long time. "I just had to sink my mental teeth into something solid," she said.

In this shaky world of ours, we can certainly understand what that girl was experiencing, for most of us have had that same need to sink our teeth into something solid. When ground seems to be breaking up beneath our feet and we're afraid of dropping into blackness, we do some mighty strange things, and very few of them do us any good. But we feel so alone, so frightened, and so uncared-for. If we can't reach upward for the things we need in our aching hearts—and if we only reach outward, this world can be a very empty place.

What is loneliness? Does it have anything to do with where you are at a particular moment? Can you be lonely in a crowd?

I don't know about you, but I'm not always lonely when I'm all by myself. Like many other people, I can keep myself busy with thoughts of those who are close to me. Even if my mind were turned off, my spirit could find the company of God and Christ His Son in prayer, and I would not be lonely. I once spent some days in a simple two-room shack in a desert area of southern California, and did not know a haunting loneliness. It was different from being in a city, or even in a suburb, where I could be among people, but I didn't mind it. In fact, I found it for then a needed experience. I may find time to repeat it someday.

But I have heard some people describe the most desperate feelings of loneliness that came to them even when they were in the midst of a crowd. They may even feel it in their own homes and among their friends. In a sense, they're out there in the middle of a spiritual desert all the time, and they don't find anything enjoyable about it— in fact, they're miserable!

Once there was an elderly minister who decided to pay a visit to a very old lady who couldn't get to most of the church services any more. She had lived an interesting life, had known many friends, and enjoyed a long and successful career in business; but the time had come for her to retire, and gradually her friends had died or moved away. She was very lonely and was therefore quite delighted to see her minister. They had a wonderful visit, chatting together and sharing many memories of their acquaintances in the congregation, but eventually the minister looked at his watch and saw that it was time for him to get back to his study. He picked up his hat from the hall table and motioned the old woman not to get up from her chair. He said good-bye, shook hands with her, and leaned down to kiss her cheek lightly. The woman's face glowed with happiness as she looked up at him. "Thank you," she whispered, "thank you—you see, nobody ever kisses me any more."

There are so many other folks who feel this way. They

have no one to give them a kiss on the cheek or any other
sign of caring, and this is perhaps the real meaning of
loneliness. It's a sort of distance that comes between
people, even when they're standing, living, working only
inches apart. And yet, we can be out on a hilltop, far from
any form of human life, and still find no distance between
us and the people we know and love.

How many lonely people do you know? Did you ever
stop and think that you shouldn't know any? If you really
cared about everyone you know, that in itself would help
to wipe out any hurtful loneliness they might feel,
wouldn't it? Somebody ought to care about the world's
lonely people—Somebody wants *us* to care.

## 9. The Open Road Is Closing—Fast!

It's funny how a little bit of neglect can go such a long way. A line of automobiles may be gliding over a smooth, four-lane highway, until one driver lets his attention wander from the road in front of him. Maybe he allows himself to daydream for a moment—we've all done that at one time or another—and suddenly there's a horrible grinding of metal on metal, rubber on concrete, and glass breaking into hundreds of pieces. One driver's moment of neglect can cost any number of lives.

We do a lot of thinking—but not nearly enough—about what it means to drive these cars on our roads today. Stop and consider it—every time you get in your car, you put yourself in command of a weapon that weighs a couple of tons, give or take a pound or two. You're a keg of dynamite, in a sense.

Did you ever notice that people often behave differently when they get behind a steering wheel? The nicest guy in the world may turn out to be a real villain on the highway—and watch out for those little old ladies who suddenly become unguided missles on their way to the supermarket! Psychologists have come up with dozens of theories about the change that takes place in us when we drive our cars, but whatever it is, it isn't very good, according to the traffic fatality figures. We seem to sense a power that we don't ordinarily feel in our homes, or our jobs, and we become careless. We daydream, or we try to solve our problems, and some of us let off steam and cuss at the first provocation—*and we kill people!* We don't mean to do it, and we'd do just about anything to undo it, but it's too late.

A short time ago, on a perfectly beautiful day, I was driving along a Wisconsin highway, when I noticed that the cars in front of me were beginning to slow down, and I felt a chill go through me. I guess most of us expect to see an accident at a time like that—at least I did —and I braced myself for the worst.

What a relief! There wasn't any accident, after all. The cars were slowing down because the road ahead began to get narrower, and we had to form fewer lanes. It was a squeeze, nothing more, and I actually felt grateful to be inching ahead so slowly.

Then I saw a flash of a bright color from the corner of my eye, and before I could glance in the rearview mirror, a convertible shot out of the line of cars behind me, whizzed past on the shoulder of the road, and cut in front of me into an impossibly small amount of space. In fact, if I hadn't stopped in complete astonishment, I would have slammed right into that car, and I don't have to tell you what a big lump I felt in my throat when I realized it.

I couldn't help hoping that a policeman had seen what happened. Apparently none did. I squinted in the bright sun and took a good look at the people who were in that convertible, expecting, I suppose, to find some pretty wild characters. What a surprise! There in the front seat was Mr. Average, as nice a man as you might ever expect to see, and next to him was Mrs. Average, a very pleasant-looking woman. On the back seat were three fine, handsome children, side by side—plenty of reason for any man to care with all his heart about what became of them. That might have been the last day in the lives of all of those people. In one careless, reckless, unthinking moment, a father might have cut off the future of his entire family! Those were mighty uncomfortable thoughts, and they gave me a strange feeling, but apparently they hadn't occurred to the laughing, jolly family in the car ahead of me.

I guess my halo was getting a bit tight at that moment, because I remembered something I certainly had wanted to forget. I remembered a time when I was stopped for speeding on a nice open road, and fined twenty-three dollars for my carelessness. I had been daydreaming, but I didn't even want to mention that to the traffic court judge because I felt ashamed of myself for allowing it to happen.

Maybe some of us get a little sick of hearing all those slogans about safe driving, and we're beginning to make fun of some of them—but they make sense, and we often don't. We have to face the fact that there aren't many wide-open spaces left on our highways, and we'll just have to give up our desire to drive our cars as fast as they can possibly go. There are more cars on the roads every day, and we can expect to see a great many more in the years ahead. And what are we as a nation going to do about those crowded conditions on our highways? Get more and more angry? Drive faster and faster every time we see an inch of space ahead of us? Buy more powerful automobiles that can leap in and out of traffic? That's what we'll do if we keep on ignoring the problem; but at the risk of adding one more slogan to the list, I'd like to point out that our carelessness can kill us.

How many times have you said, "Somebody ought to put a light at that corner?" Many more streets need them, especially as you get into the more densely populated areas of the country. The old traffic lights aren't enough, and the number of accidents that happen only two blocks from home will confirm that. But some of us don't want more traffic lights because they make us stop our high-powered cars for a minute or two. We don't like stop-streets, one-way streets, and some of us even get annoyed with the officials we appoint to help our children get safely across the streets. As a matter of fact, we're getting mighty upset about the whole problem of traffic congestion—just give us that old open road where we can press our foot down on the accelerator and let 'er rip! So there we are, out on the highway, looking for lots of room and not finding any, and we're just about ready to explode when we run into a traffic jam. It seems that everybody else wanted to get out on the open road, too, and they're all boiling mad.

I never like to look at the number of traffic accidents reported in the newspapers after a holiday weekend, do you? We don't have to. We can let the paper stay folded and unread—and many of us do. But I think most of us realize that we can't go on living—and killing—this way much longer.

## 10.   Home Is Where the Hurt Is

Two men were discussing their marriages, and one of them was heard to say, "You know, Fred, life used to be very sweet when Joan and I were first married. I would come home from work, and there was Joan, waiting for me at the door with my slippers; and there was the dog, jumping up and down and barking." He shook his head and sighed, "It's all changed, now, though." "In what way?" his friend asked. "Well," the first man said, "Now I come home from work—and Joan barks at me and the dog waits with my slippers." His friend smiled wisely. "I wouldn't complain if I were you," he said, "you're still getting the same service, aren't you?"

Like so many jokes about family life today, it contains some truths. Something is causing all those divorces in our country, and one of the most frequent complaints from any husband or wife is that the other one has "changed."

Since so many people seem to care about nothing but their own lives, you'd think their families would be in good shape, but that, unhappily, isn't the picture of the American home. It's in trouble, deep trouble, and we're all a little uneasy about it. We see our neighbors' marriages go down the drain, one after the other, and some of their married children aren't getting off to a good start, either, and they're just plain worried.

The homes that nourish a nation's young form the backbone of that nation—in a sense, they are forming the future for all of us. Many psychiatrists hold different opinions about the effect of environment on a human being, but most lay people are pretty sure that it's one of the most important influences in anyone's life.

Recently I read about a tragic mistake that had been made in a hospital in Austria fifteen years ago. Two young women had given birth to baby girls on the same day, and somehow the infants were put in the wrong cribs. They were switched, and no one realized it at the time. When both mothers were ready to go home, they carried their newborn babies, completely unaware that they were holding someone else's child. The mistake wasn't discovered until the girls were in their teens, but by then the damage had been done.

One girl had been brought up in a loving home where she also had the advantages of a good education and comfortable surroundings. She had good food to eat, attractive clothes to wear, and warm friends. She was a very fine young lady.

The other girl had been taken home to a world of poverty, misery, and degradation. Her mother was unmarried, and the stigma was transferred to the daughter by the other people in the community—a very unkind, but common, attitude. The girl rarely had enough to eat, she wore cast-off rags, and she was totally uneducated. Is it any surprise that she was a wretched, unhappy person by the time the mistake was discovered?

So, you see, our homes mean a great deal to our young —and to us, too, for that matter. People can take a lot of abuse from this old world as long as they can find comfort, love, and warmth in their homes. God had a good reason for setting ". . . the solitary in families" (PSALM 68:6, KJV).

What's going on in our homes today? Those that aren't

breaking up are breaking down on the inside, where it doesn't always show right away. Any minister can tell you that he hears more and more complaints every day, and still he can't find out who's to blame.

I knew a nice young couple who really had me baffled for a while. First the husband came to see me, and we had a long talk in my study. He was terribly upset, but unlike some distressed people, he seemed willing to take the blame for his marital troubles.

"It's all my fault," he said, and I could see the pain in his heart glaring right out of his eyes. "You can't blame Ruth for running away, not after what I did to her."

"All right," I said, "tell me exactly what you've done, and maybe we can find a way to fix things up."

"Well," the husky young man said, turning his face away in shame, "I used to be a captain in the Marine Corps, and I guess I just sort of forgot myself now and then after I got out—whenever we used to argue, that is. I'd get pretty mad, and—well—I guess I used to slap Ruth a couple of times. So she left me—and she was right!"

He really did have a problem! "Where is she now?" I asked, and he shook his head. He didn't know. He couldn't go out looking for his wife—feeling the way he did—and so I went, and I was able to find her by talking to her relatives, who weren't very happy about the separation, either. They promised to do all they could to help the two young people repair their marriage, if only they would agree to try. Well, that's where my job began.

I made an appointment with Joe and Ruth, and he arrived first. He was extremely nervous, and I wondered how I would ever pry that load of guilt off his back, even with his wife's help—which I wasn't sure I would get.

Then the door opened and Ruth came in, rather quietly at first—until she saw her husband and went after him! She literally riddled him with a stream of angry words that came from her mouth like machine-gun bullets, and I began to realize that the problem in this marriage was big enough for both of them to share.

I sat back and waited for Ruth to run out of breath, and that didn't happen for a long time. "You know, Ruth," I said, when she finally calmed down, "I was foolish enough to believe that it was all Joe's fault, just as he claimed it was. But nobody in this world could live with a mouth like yours. The trouble with both of you is that neither of you has a self that's really fit to live with."

That's the trouble with so many of us—we just aren't always fit to live with, yet blame somebody else for making life miserable. We feel we've been short-changed in our relationships with people—whether in marriage, business, community, or any other area of life—and we decide to get even by short-changing everyone else. That's an unhappy way to live, and the world is starting to show the results of it.

How is your family these days? Is it going through a rough time, or is everything smooth and harmonious? Do you know whether anyone in your family has problems, or don't you want to interfere in their lives? Maybe that's just what they need—someone who kindly, and very wisely, cares.

## 11. Life on a Punch-Card

It's no surprise that people feel as if they're lost in the shuffle these days. This is a funny kind of world—full of digits, symbols, formulas, and strange-sounding words —and sometimes we have a hard time understanding each other. Have you ever looked over your son's shoulder when he was doing his homework? Then you know what it is to feel out of step with things. A mother and father used to find comfort in the thought that they could guide their children—at least part of the way in life— because they had the benefit of experience in the world. But now everything is new, changed, different, and even our experience is old-fashioned!

I wouldn't be surprised if scientists discovered that one of modern man's worst problems is with numbers. We certainly have a lot of them, in all kinds of combinations, and if a man doesn't have a fantastic memory, he can run into trouble. When a man gets up in the morning, he has to check his calendar to find out what day of what month of what year it is—plain old Monday or Tuesday won't do. He has to be precise, because somewhere, sometime, during the day—at least once—he'll probably have to record today's date on a piece of paper that will go into a file where it will be checked by a mechanical instrument and put away for future reference.

Our man's day has just begun, but already his brain is clicking away. He may have to catch a bus or train to go to work, and he'd better remember the number of it and the exact time of departure so that he can get to where he wants to go. If he has a job that doesn't deal directly with numbers, he's still not off the hook because our entire modern society is gradually beginning to function strictly according to numbers. We're living in the age of the computer, and I think most of us are just a little afraid that we ourselves might turn into numbers.

Nevertheless, those numbers make life not only convenient but downright comfortable at times, and we're beginning to realize that we can no longer get along without them. In a country this size, populated by so many millions of people, it's amazing that we can send letters from one coast to another in a matter of a day or two. I must admit that I don't understand exactly how the zip code system works, and I can never remember my number, but I can't object to having my mail delivered faster. I love to open a letter!

Numbers protect us, too, and if you've ever had the opportunity to see computers at work in police laboratories and files, you know what a warm feeling of security they can give you.

No, numbers haven't overwhelmed us, even though it sometimes seems that way. Actually, they're supposed to keep us from getting lost in the shuffle—they hold our place in line. Just imagine what would happen if there weren't any records of us anywhere! How would anyone get in touch with us? What would happen to us if we became so ill that we couldn't get out of bed to summon aid? What would happen to the money we had saved for our old age if we simply put it in the bank, filed under our names? It may be an uncomfortable realization, but many people may have exactly the same name we have, and how would a bank tell us apart? These are only small examples—and I can't go into more complicated ones because I don't know enough about mathematics—but they serve to remind us that numbers help us to hold onto our identity in a world full of people.

But life on a punch-card can be very trying at times, especially when the computers go haywire. I read about a woman who kept getting a bill from an oil company, even though she had paid the amount due some months earlier. Very patiently, she wrote a letter to the oil company and returned the bill each month after it came in the mail, but more bills kept coming—complete with those long, smooth, cream-covered cards full of holes and numbers, and instructions not to "mutilate, bend, fold, or staple." Finally the woman lost her patience and in her frustration seized the card and folded it over and over into something that looked like an accordion. That made her feel better, somehow. Then she got a stapler and stamped the card with as many staples as it would hold, and when she had added a few snips with a scissor, she carefully addressed the envelope to the oil company, enclosed the hardly recognizable card without a word of explanation, sealed the envelope, and mailed it. She never heard from the company again.

Don't we all wish we could do something like that now and again! Maybe it approaches the feeling we have when we want to take off for the hills and forget about the whole computerized world. Life seems to be getting so impersonal, so over-organized. We miss the sense of challenge we used to feel, the sense of things to be conquered, and we wonder whether the world is running short of opportunities.

We all have to make some difficult adjustments in life, and we shouldn't be too quick to point a finger if we see a lot of Adams taking refuge within themselves. No, they haven't really stopped loving life, or the world, or their fellow man, but they're pretty mixed up about where they fit in with the rest of us.

## 12. Our Crowded, Noisy Planet

It was four o'clock in the afternoon in New York City, and a taxi driver turned to the man who had climbed into the back seat, "Why did you want a cab, Mister? You can get across town a lot faster by walking!" And out on a freeway near Chicago during rush hour, a truck driver pulled off the road by a lunchroom and went inside for a cup of coffee. "I'm just going to stay here until they all go home!" he told the waitress angrily.

Ours is a crowded world and it's getting more crowded every day. We hear some pretty depressing facts about the population explosion, but what can we do about it? We have to go on living—don't we?—even if life becomes one big traffic jam.

I had a very frustrating experience not long ago, and it's one that almost everybody else has known at some time in his life. I was driving from Palm Desert to Anaheim, California, for a speaking engagement, and I had started out early so that I wouldn't have to worry if I was delayed in the traffic. I had no trouble getting as far as Riverside, but just then the sportscar races ended and crowds of cars began to fill the road. It took me two-and-a-half hours to go thirty-four miles, and most of that time was spent sitting in my car, eating the exhaust from the car in front of me, and not moving an inch! At a time like that, we want to drive right through the fields at the side of the road—anywhere, as long as it's away from people!

Russell Baker recently commented on our fast-moving society when he mentioned one of the latest developments on the Lackawanna Railroad, a line that carries many metropolitan commuters back and forth between their jobs and homes. It seems the railroad added a special convenience for commuters—a car was set aside for religious services, complete with pastor, so that, as Russell Baker put it, people could commune and commute at the same time.

America is really a country on the move. We can drive into almost anything today—from a movie to a bank— and although some of us may look upon these "conveniences" as slightly ghastly, we have to admit that many of them are necessary. Ours has been called a "leisure-time" world, yet most of us never have a minute to spare, and we can save precious moments by driving to a store and making our purchase without getting out of the car. We may feel that we ought to draw the line when it comes to religion, but there's no reason why we should leave our souls behind in our mad dash around the world, is there? I'm thinking of one church in particular, in St. Petersburg, Florida, where there simply wasn't enough room inside the church for all the people who came to attend the services. And so, Dr. J. Wallace Hamilton, the minister of the church, decided to invite the overflow into the church parking lot, where some microphones were set up to convey the audible part of the service. This church has now become famous for its welcome to the traveler as well as to the permanent resident, for its invitation to men and women on wheels— and they need God every bit as much as those on foot or on a bench or in a pew!

It takes time for us to get used to all these new things, and time is something we don't have in large amounts.

Oh, yes, we're going somewhere, but sometimes we're not quite sure where or why. As one man said when he was asked where the world was going, "We're all going to the gas pump."

We don't mind the hustle and bustle most of the time, but some days are special and we don't like to observe them with so much fuss. Christmas is one of these days, and Easter is another. Don't we all grit our teeth around the first of November and say that this year we're going to do things differently? This year we aren't going to get caught up in the awful commercial rush that doesn't seem to have anything at all to do with Christmas! And then what happens? Before you know it, you go out to get one little gift—just something simple—and you're trapped! You find yourself pushing through the crowded aisles of stores filled to the bursting point with glittering merchandise, and trying to get the attention of a salesclerk who's trying to handle six customers at one time. Then there's the marketing, the wrapping of gifts, the mailing of cards, the tree to be decorated, and the baking! You wonder whether it's really worth all of this —and yet, you wouldn't have wanted to miss the important parts of it.

You may be thinking that Christmas got lost in the rush, when suddenly everything comes to a halt. Perhaps you just got home, that final gift tucked under your arm, or perhaps you just took the pumpkin pie out of the oven—and you notice that a hush has fallen over the world. Wherever you are, you can sense it, and other people sense it, too, and they stop whatever they're doing. They're listening to their heartbeat—their soul-beat!—and they're quietly, reverently celebrating the birth of the Son of God.

In another day or two, we're all back in our frenzied

world-on-wheels, going who-knows-where, but a trace of sadness lingers in our hearts. Why can't we stop more often? Why can't we get off by ourselves more often and spend some time with God? How can He possibly keep up with all of us in our madly spinning world?

I think some wise families have recognized the importance of moments of solitude, of those times when each of us has to go into a room and close the door and be alone—perhaps to pray, to think our thoughts, to ask some questions, and hope for answers. This is a shrill, high-strung world full of interruptions and distractions, and we do need to pull ourselves out of it now and then.

I travel quite a lot, and after several trips I find myself looking forward to spending an afternoon out on my patio at home where there is nothing but the desert and some distant mountains to pull at the sleeve of my thoughts. One day when I was there, half-dozing in the sunshine, I let my mind wander in any old way. It was a beautiful day; the sun was warm and bright, and the air was hardly moving. Best of all, there wasn't a sound to be heard—except for the dull booms of some jet planes over the airbase on the other side of the mountains, but they only reminded me how distant I was from crowds of people.

Then I heard a strange, irritating sound, and looked up, annoyed that my mind had to come to attention on such a day. My intruder was a tiny, curled piece of paper that was skidding back and forth across the concrete with a rasping, mocking noise. It seemed like the most insignificant thing in the world, and yet, as I thought about it, debating whether to go over and pick it up and tuck it away somewhere, it occurred to me that this little piece of paper represented the hundreds and thousands of things that disturb the peace and quiet of men's souls.

Like a lone horsefly buzzing the ears of a fisherman in the middle of a serene lake, like a single creaking timber in the roof of a cabin during the stillness of night, like an unhooked screen door tapping in the dawn breezes —this metallic, screeching world of ours breaks in upon our communion with God and we feel—perhaps only momentarily—cut off from the very meaning of our lives.

Distractions? The world is full of them, important and unimportant, harmless and destructive. Everywhere we look we see wants, necessary and unnecessary; desires, meaningful and meaningless; ambitions, worthy and unworthy; hundreds of thousands of things that fleetingly or constantly seek to attract our attention, to claim our interest, to demand our loyalties and our energies. And thus our world becomes filled with a frantic search for remedies to the nagging strains that are made upon our minds, our souls, and our lives.

How, we ask ourselves, can God get through to us, when we rarely give Him the chance?

## 13. "Scared on the Inside"

The man who sat in my office carried heavy responsibilities on his shoulders. He had an important position in a huge corporation, and he was the kind who gave his all to his work, but evidently it wasn't giving him much in return. He was very bitter, and I sat quietly while he poured out his long-buried resentments against everyone and everything. He couldn't seem to name one person he liked or one situation that didn't leave him boiling mad. All the while he talked he sat on the edge of his chair, literally tying himself into a tight knot.

When he finished, we just looked at each other, and then I said, "What are you afraid of?" I took him by surprise, I suppose, because a man of his achievements and standing wouldn't ordinarily think of himself as being afraid, and for a moment I thought that he was going to add me to his list of pet peeves. Then he sank back in his chair and let his arms drop loosely at his sides. "How do you know I'm afraid?" he asked. "Does it show that much?"

"No," I said, "not unless you've seen a lot of fear in other people, as I have. But nobody talks the way you do unless he's scared on the inside."

Sometimes people fool us. Sometimes we seem to think that we're the only ones who are scared, and we marvel at people who can go through the most trying experiences without batting an eye. Nothing seems to upset them, to get to them, to shake them up, even a little. But is this true? Are some of us heroes and some of us cowards? I don't think so, and the more I discover about human nature, the more I realize that we all feel frightened at some times in our lives. We just show it in different ways.

These are certainly frightening days for just about everbody in the world. We never know what's going to happen next; and when you consider the events that some of us—perhaps those of us in the middle of life—have lived through, you can understand why we feel that way. We've seen the human race try to blow up the earth more than once, and we have good reason to worry—because now there's a bomb big enough to finish the job.

Particularly during the past year or two I have sensed more insecurities, fears, frustrations, loneliness, and apathy in more people than ever before. We human beings have put together much of the material parts of our world, but now we find that something is missing. Our deepest needs are just not being met.

But we can also see so many good things in our world and we keep telling ourselves that everything will turn out all right. People are living longer because so many diseases have been wiped out or reduced in intensity, more people can read and write and therefore communicate with each other, many of us are financially secure, our children are going to get a fine education, and, all in all, we can't complain.

That's just the trouble—we don't know what's bothering us and so we can't gripe about it. When we can get something off our chests we usually feel better, but many of our fears don't seem to come to the surface where we can do something about them. They stay curled up inside us, where they begin to ache and ache. Ask any psychiatrist—and even many medical doctors—and you'll learn that people are suffering a lot of pain these days, even though they aren't crying out.

To make matters worse, some of us take out our frustrations on those around us, and then we feel guilty about it—and we should, because it isn't fair to hurt someone else just because we've been hurt.

The next time somebody picks on you, take a good look at him. Watch his eyes and see if you don't find a trace of fear in them. He may have something in common with you—he may be just as scared of life as you are!

## 14.  Running in the Wrong Direction

A good many years ago—more than I care to think about, perhaps—when I was going to college, I had a summer job as a salesman, and I had an experience that has stayed with me all these years. I was in a little town along the Tennessee River, calling on a hardware store owner, and as we were talking I heard a strange musical sound coming from down the street. I tried to keep my mind on our conversation, but the music became louder and louder and more and more intriguing. It sounded like a calliope.

The store owner saw that my attention was wandering and he smiled. "That's the *Majestic*," he explained, with a touch of pride in his voice. "She'll be pulling up to the dock in a few minutes." The *Majestic* was the last remaining showboat to sail up and down an American river, and the sight of it coming around the bend toward the dock was something I didn't want to miss. Neither did my prospective customer, and he took me down to the dock with him. Both of us felt like two children as we watched that beautiful old boat tie up at its berth.

I had planned to spend the night in another town across the river, but my customer very graciously invited me to stay with him and his family so that we could pay a visit to the showboat that evening. Naturally I was delighted, not only because I would see a real, honest-to-goodness showboat, but because I was hungry for the company of friendly people.

Everything lived up to my expectations, and I felt as though I had stepped into the past when we went aboard the *Majestic*. Even Captain Reynolds, a warm, wonderful old gentleman, looked exactly right standing up there on the rear deck, and we stopped to talk with him for a while. Then I noticed the river—it was going the wrong way, and I remarked about it to Captain Reynolds.

"Oh, no," he explained, "You forgot that the Tennessee River flows north through this part of the country. It's not that the river is wrong—you are."

Some people turn and run in the wrong direction, too, and sometimes they don't realize what they're doing. I don't think any sports fans will forget the time when big Jim Marshall of the Minnesota Vikings football team picked up the ball and ran as fast as he could down the field toward the goalpost—but the wrong goalpost! Some of the other players tried to stop him, but Jim avoided them. It was a brilliant run, but all for nothing, and Jim was pretty embarrassed. However, it really didn't hurt anyone or cause any heartache. The Vikings even won the ball game.

But life isn't always that kind, and we can't always laugh at our mistakes. Sometimes the wrong way can do us a lot of harm, and we may not be able to turn around once we get started in that direction. Douglas Corrigan won fame as "Wrong-Way Corrigan" when he flew his plane in the wrong direction, but think of the pilots who lost their lives because they didn't stay on course.

We're not necessarily going to arrive somewhere simply because we're moving. We may be running at full speed in the wrong direction, and this may have a lot to do with the troubles in our lives. Sometimes we think the river is running upstream, when all the time it's we

who may be wrong—even if we're standing still, we may
be facing in the wrong direction. It might be good to
think about this when we're inclined to shrug our shoulders and turn our backs on the world. Is that the way
we should be facing, or are we going off in the wrong direction? Is the trouble out there in the rest of the world,
or is it in our very own hearts?

## 15.  His Price Was Too High

People came from everywhere to visit the New York World's Fair, but one little boy's visit made headlines. He had asked his parents many times to take him to the Fair, and they kept answering—absentmindedly, as many parents do—"Soon."

Well, the time came when "soon" was too long to wait, and young Dominick took off for the Fair by himself. It wasn't many miles from his home, and he took a bus to the Fair grounds, but I guess his sense of adventure overwhelmed him, because he simply didn't want to go home at the end of the day. The Fair was a dazzling sight, a city from another world, and the exhibits were marvels to a boy's mind. Nighttime was even better, with colorfully lighted fountains that shot columns of vapor up into the sky. No, he had to stay, and amazingly he found the means to do it—for eleven days. When Dominick was hungry, he picked some coins out of a "wishing well" exhibit and bought hamburgers and hot dogs; he washed himself in one of the fountains after everyone had gone home; at night he slept in a lifeboat in one of the displays.

During the eleven days this young man was having the time of his life, his parents were in torment. As soon as they discovered his absence, they reported it to the police, who in turn issued a seventeen-state alarm. All kinds of frightening thoughts went through the parents' minds—from kidnapping to murder, and we can under-

62

stand their relief when they heard that their boy had been found, perfectly safe, at the Fair.

Some of us can chuckle over these antics. "He's just a boy," we'll say, and perhaps a few of us will admire his daring. It reminds us of Huck Finn, and you just don't find that kind of boy any more. But I wonder if Dominick really had such a good time, after all. I wonder if he didn't stay so long at the Fair because he didn't want to go home and face his parents. Maybe he *forced* himself to have a good time so that he wouldn't have to admit to himself that he was wrong to leave home.

Aren't we just as wrong to leave home? And isn't that exactly what we're doing when we run off in any direction except the one that leads back to God? People don't really have to keep running—they could come to a stop, think over their lives, and come back to where they belong. But somehow they don't want to do it. Why?

Man seems to be carrying a chip on his shoulder, and I think he put it there when he left Eden. He seems to blame God for all his misfortunes. He doesn't exactly want to cut himself off from God—that would be too drastic—but he doesn't like the demands God makes on him.

Take happiness, for example. God promises us peace —*if* we live according to His will. But modern man doesn't want any "ifs." He wants to push a button and be happy—just like that, instant joy, ready-made fulfillment! Never mind all this business about "Let us love one another"—that was for another generation, not ours!

We don't have time to live the Beatitudes or to listen to the Sermon on the Mount, and we can't sit still long enough to partake of the Lord's Supper. We want our rewards right now! We insist on being happy, constantly and without interruption, and we resent anything or anyone that threatens this numbness we call "bliss."

But God has other plans for us. He seems to think we ought to have a lot more to do with each other. He says we should sympathize with each other, help each other, feel each other's sorrows as deeply as our own, and exult in each other's joy. Now, that's a pretty big order. It calls for a lot of our time, our thought, our concern, and mostly our love, and we aren't always willing to give them. We need these resources for our own lives, don't we? Besides, we're just too busy for that sort of life. God is asking too much of us—the price of His kind of happiness is too high, and we'll just have to look elsewhere.

And so we try to find happiness in some other way, and what do we get? Precious little, or nothing at all. Happiness doesn't exist in a vacuum; it needs the uneven, high-and-low rhythm of real life, not some smooth, glossy substitute. Happiness isn't a tranquilizer, either; it's one of the most powerful stimulators in the world because it makes us more sensitive to other people and their feelings. We care; and because we care, we do. We get sweat on the brow of our soul and wrinkles of care on our heart—and we're truly, deeply happy. This is God's kind of happiness, and there isn't any other kind.

Some of us haven't realized this yet. We're still carrying that chip around on our shoulders because we think God let us down. We claim that He didn't keep His promises, but we didn't keep to the Way that led to the promises, so where does that leave us? We've gone off to the Fair by ourselves and we don't want to admit that we've done something wrong by going alone. We're trying to justify our behavior by saying we're having a great old time, a real adventure, but isn't it true that deep in our hearts we're hoping that Someone will find us here among this vast crowd of other runaway children?

## 16. "Let's Make Our Own!"

How far can we run away from God? That's an interesting question, and we can answer it in several different ways, depending upon our definition of the word "progress."

Many people think we have come a long way, strictly on our own powers. Take a look at our world, and you'll see how man has changed the face of it through the centuries. Why, we're even beginning to change our own appearances because we've learned so much about nourishment and the effects of certain foods upon the development of the human body. We're also daring to probe the space around our earth, perhaps with the thought of changing that, too, once we learn a little more about it. Yes, we've come very far.

We're living in a do-it-yourself age when people make what they want. It all started after World War II when so many homes had to be built for the families of men who were returning to civilian life. There weren't enough skilled craftsmen to go around, so some of us had to learn how to use a hammer and a few other tools. Then came power tools and the workshop in the basement, and now there's hardly anything we won't tackle! If we need a new garage, we can go out and buy the parts in a kit, complete with step-by-step instructions for putting it together. If our water pipes leak, we try our hand at weekend plumbing. In short, we are self-contained, self-reliant, self-confident people.

Our great metropolitan cities are probably the most impressive examples of our technological skill, and we have good reason to be proud of them. Our cities have their faults, to be sure, but they're beautiful sights from the window of a plane—whether they're reflecting the sun's light from their millions of glass panes, or sparkling merrily in the night's blackness. When you see them from street level, you may notice that some of the buildings could use some improvements, but some of those skyscrapers are works of contemporary art that can snatch away the breath of a man who stands looking up at them.

The trouble with man-made things is that they don't hold up under some of the demands we make on them. On November 9, 1965, the city of New York—the largest in the world—came to a dead stop when the lights went out right in the middle of the 5:30 evening rush hour. Somewhere up in a power plant in Ontario, Canada, something went wrong with an electrical relay system, and a phenomenal blackout began to cover most of the northeast coast.

Now, most of us would have to admit that we're mighty dependent upon electrical power, and that when that power is shut off, life can be somewhat uncomfortable. But we get candles out of the cupboard, strike a match, and make the best of it until the current is turned on again. Not so in the city of New York—or in any other great metropolitan center, for that matter—where a blackout is a major crisis.

Millions of people came to a stop when the power went off, and many of them found themselves in dangerous predicaments. Some were trapped in elevators, between floors; thousands were down in subway tunnels, between stations; and thousands more found themselves groping their way through darkened streets filled with cars gone wild because the traffic lights had stopped working. It was frightening. I happened to be in New York that night, and I saw a look of fear on the faces I saw in the light cast by candles, matches, flashlights, and flashbulbs. People had suddenly realized that their man-made material world could go wrong, and it shook them up. They began to huddle together, to reach out toward each other in the darkness, because they didn't want to be alone with their fears.

This is always the plight of men who try to set themselves up as their own gods. When the lights go out, there isn't anything they can do, except stop what they're doing, stand still, and hope that help will come.

As a nation we experienced a sort of blackout in our hearts a year ago when our young, vigorous President was assassinated. John F. Kennedy was a man of great achievement and promise, a man who was guarded night and day—yet he was cut down by something as small and ugly and man-made as a lead bullet fired from the barrel of a cheap, man-made metal rifle. In the days of our mourning, we began to realize that our tools could be turned upon us, and we knew that we were vulnerable.

But some of us haven't learned our lesson. We keep looking for a substitute for God because we haven't lost our desire to belong to something greater than we are. We must give ourselves over to something. We don't want to care about anyone or anything, but somebody, something, *must* care about us!

## 17.  This Suicide of Success

Not long ago I was talking to the president of a large corporation that employed over 30,000 people. We were sitting in his office, and there was something about that vast, comfortably furnished room that told me I was talking to a very powerful person. He was also completely honest.

"You know, Rube," he said, "I've been with this company for thirty-seven years, now. I've held just about every kind of job in it, from the bottom right on up here to the top. I've been president for the past three years, and I can tell you that they've been the three most agonizing years of my life."

These words came from a man who really loved his job. He literally lived for his career and he wasn't about to give it up. He had found something bigger than he was, something in which he could lose himself, and although it might eventually shorten his life, it gave it some meaning—in his eyes.

Later that morning, on my way out of the building, I ran into the president's assistant, whom I had met before, and we stopped to talk for a few minutes. Here was another man who enjoyed his work, and he obviously admired his boss because he spoke of him with deep respect. "I'll tell you a secret," he said, and he smiled a bit sheepishly, "I'm not smart enough to move into that big office up there—but even if I were, you couldn't get me to be president of any company, not for all the money in the world!"

It was certainly a morning for contrasts. "Why?" I asked.

"Maybe there's something wrong with me," he said, and his expression was serious. "I know I'm not lazy, and I want to get ahead as much as anybody. But I'll have to stop somewhere short of the top—there's too much responsibility in that job up there!"

I think that young assistant was wise to draw the line where he did. He must have sensed that he would have to make some big sacrifices if he went much further, and there were some things he didn't want to give up. He had a wife and a fine little boy, and together they had a happy life—was any job worth that much?

Plenty of successful people have families, too, but sometimes they have to play second fiddle to a career, and this can break up a home in a very short time. Not every wife can tolerate such competition, and even children resent a job that takes more of dad's loyalty than they do.

It's easy to say that a man should be able to handle a home as well as a demanding career, but it's another thing to do it. A key executive position isn't an ordinary job that lasts from nine to five, five or six days a week, with two weeks' vacation with pay. It lasts twenty-four hours a day and calls for every last ounce of energy, judgment, intuition, education, and dedication that a man can muster. And sometimes it calls for his mind, body, and soul, as well—and many of us can't say "no" when we should. This is when our careers offer their greatest temtation to us; this is when they become something bigger than we are; this is when we begin to think we've found a substitute for God.

Success was meant to be a part of life, not all of it,

69

but there are many lonely, troubled people high up in those plush offices who have come to understand this too late. They don't know how to go back along the road by which they came to their lofty heights, and so they must go on—making those decisions that will change the lives of thousands of people and consume millions of dollars and earn, hopefully, many millions more.

Just let those men make a few mistakes, and their imitation god will toss them right off the peak of their achievement. Would you like to make decisions under those conditions?

Moral values can change when success lays a hand on them, and many a man has had to shift his principles around in order to keep his illustrious job. Some men can't do it. I knew one who was faced with the kind of dilemma that cuts a person in two, and I found myself wishing I could offer him a painless way out of it. But I couldn't, and he wouldn't have come to me if he hadn't wanted to face up to his problem. He was an executive caught in one of those complicated stock battles that occasionally make financial news. No one was displeased with the way he had done his job, but he held a key position that was valuable to each side that was fighting to control his company, and both sides wanted to get him out of the way so that they could attempt to get their own men in. It was a rough struggle, and all the rules of fair play were thrown out the window, and the man who came to talk to me was trying to make up his mind about his own set of rules. "They're tapping my telephone," he said, "hoping to hear something they can hold over my head. And now they've spread these rumors about my health—even my friends are beginning to think I've got a serious illness." He shook his head. "If I'm going to fight this thing," he said, loosening his tie and running his finger around the inside of his neat white collar, "I'll have to play a dirty game, too. I'll have to get even rougher than they are."

He didn't want to fight that way, and that was the one hope for him, as far as I could see. I had seen these struggles before, and I knew that no one really won them, especially the so-called "victors."

"Don't do it, Fred," I said. "If you have to fight, do it the same way you've lived all these years—clean. Somehow you've managed to hold onto your integrity and a very important job at the same time, and I guess you'll have to choose between them now. And I don't think you want to give up that integrity of yours!"

You can guess how the story ended when Fred decided that he had no use for rumor-spreading and listening in on private conversations. Yes, he did lose his job, and it cost him more than a large salary. He was a proud man, and the loss of his job humiliated him. He was hurt, too, because he knew he didn't deserve the dismissal. But he wasn't bitter—and he might have been if he had made the wrong decision. "I made the right choice," he told me later, and his face relaxed into a boyish smile. "And you have no idea how relieved I feel!" He had troubles, plenty of them, but at least they were all outside him. He still had his soul.

Now and then, perhaps only for a fleeting moment, people who have dedicated their lives to success must have to stop and think about the emptiness of their lives. They have such a tremendous influence on so many people, yet they never allow themselves to get involved with them. They can't, because they've forgotten how to do it. They've given up so much that was warm, close, and precious to them in order to worship their god, and they don't like to remember it. But they can't really

71

forget the days gone by, the days when they belonged to themselves, to their families, and the real God. And if, sometimes, a memory comes back to haunt them, to bring moisture to their eyes and a sob to their throats, they needn't be ashamed—no one will hear them weeping in those soundproof offices.

## 18. "Doesn't He Have Enough Money?"

Why are our children in such trouble, even though many of us talk about how much we love them? Some of us claim that we don't have time to think of anyone but our families, and yet we don't seem to be able to help them.

A fourteen-year-old retarded boy from Chicago was abandoned in a Miami air terminal by his mother, who said she loved him too much to see him suffer. The boy had been left retarded by an attack of encephalitis during his infancy, and his mother was evidently unable to accept the reality of his affliction and make the best of it. She fought against it for years, and finally she gave up.

According to the boy's older sister, his mother had announced to the family that she was taking him to a special school in Florida, and no one suspected her motives because she had always been a very doting, affectionate mother. She and the boy left Chicago by plane, and within a few days the woman returned, alone, to her home. Naturally, the family thought the boy was in the care of specialists who might help him to lead a more useful life, and they were happy for him. Little did they know the terror that must have gone through his young heart when he found himself abandoned, and unable to communicate with the strangers who tried to help him.

The police in Miami were marvelously efficient and within days they managed to trace the boy's mother, who gave them an astonishing reason for her behavior. She had been able to cope with her son's needs when he was just a little boy, she said, but now that he was older his needs were more complicated. He needed special training in forms of communication, and this was beyond her. She couldn't go through with it! She left him in the airport, hoping that he would be found by someone who would "take an interest in him."

Now that's hard to believe, but it's made more understandable by the fact that the boy's mother was evidently nearing a breakdown. She was sent to a hospital, where she was to undergo psychiatric tests.

Some other alarming things are happening between parents and children these days, and I'm afraid they all can't come under the heading of "Severe Emotional Strain." For instance, when the police in Miami were trying to learn the identity of the retarded boy, they issued his description to neighboring states—and they were besieged by telephone calls and letters from parents of missing children! And some of them had been missing for months! Most of us sit on pins and needles when our children are ten minutes late for dinner, and we can't imagine how we would feel if they didn't show up all night. How can parents manage to handle it at all when their children are missing?

We've heard many law enforcement officials say that too many parents don't know where their children are when they're not in school, and for a long time I thought that was an exaggeration. But I've come to believe it because I've seen some results of it. I live near one of those towns teen-agers and college students like to visit on long holidays such as Easter and Christmas, and I've been absolutely appalled by the number of young people who are permitted to go off on their own at a time when most families look forward to getting together. These kids are awfully young to be whooping it up in a strange town, but they have plenty of money in their pockets and I have to assume that they came not only with parental approval but with parental dollars, too. They're nice kids, and most of them come from nice homes, but they're terribly restless. Something is eating at them, and whatever it is, it certainly boils over when they get together. Quite a number of towns have been all but demolished by their collective fury.

I felt sorry for one young boy who was found unconscious in the front seat of a car. It took the police quite a while to get to him because the car was locked and they had to break their way in, but when they did, they saw that the car belonged to the boy and was not—as they had thought at first—stolen. They also found fifteen-hundred dollars in his coat pocket and a number of credit cards in his wallet. The boy had had so much to drink that he had passed out cold and had to be taken to a hospital for treatment, but in the meantime, the police got his address—a house in Beverly Hills—and they called his parents. The boy's father answered the phone, and when the police told him how they had found his son, he snapped, "Well, what's the problem? Doesn't he have enough money?"

The one thing we do give to our children today is money—very few of them have to go without it—and I'm not so sure this is doing them a bit of good. I don't think any of us want to deprive our children of anything; in fact, we all want them "to have more than I did," and we have the means to make that possible. But money never was a good substitute for the care that every boy and girl absolutely must have.

Some of us say that we don't understand our children,

but neither did any other parent in the history of the world—until he *tried*. Understanding doesn't come easily, especially when people are a generation apart, but it certainly is possible. There's a catch to it, naturally, and it's a big one. We have to be interested enough to want to understand our kids, to do some listening, and that's where the failure often begins.

We all say we love our children, yet some of us seem to love them from such a distance. Children need the warmth that comes from the nearness, the involvement, of parents' love. Their lives have to meet—and even collide, at times—in order to mean something to each other. We can't stuff a roll of bills into our childrens' hands, throw them the keys to the car, and then stand on the front doorstep, shouting, "I love you, darling!" as they drive farther and farther away from us.

We may be confused by the resentment and hostility that our young people are throwing up in our faces, but we'd better not stay confused. They are the world we claim to care about—and sometimes they don't think we care at all. Do we?

## 19. How's Your Image?

Too many billboards can clutter up a landscape, but now and then we see one that really gives our minds a message. One outside of a beautiful orchard proclaimed the wonders of "Apples You Can Eat in the Dark," and the slogan made me chuckle. Then I gave it more thought and realized that there was a lot of wisdom in those few words.

The billboard was telling passersby that they could trust the apples grown in that orchard. They could be sure that they would find no wormholes and no mushy spots in them—no sir! Why, those apples were so fresh and perfect that you could go right ahead and bite into them—even in the dark!

Most people like to feel that their character is just as trustworthy as apples you can eat in the dark. Character, as someone once put it, is what you and I are when nobody is looking. The only trouble is, we'd like to be exactly the same when someone *is* looking, and we don't always succeed.

You and I are no different from the rest of the world—we all want to look good to others. That's why the practice of "image-building" has spilled over from the public relations field into ordinary, everyday life. We're all concerned about our "image," about the way the world sees us, and we sometimes go to ridiculous lengths to impress people.

I don't think we want to build an image in order to

deceive anybody, and I don't think we're trying to fool ourselves, either. We may go a bit too far trying to dress up the facts of our lives, but we do it for a very understandable reason—nobody wants to be the "bad guy." We all want to be the "good guys" in the eyes of others, because we really, sincerely, hope that we're "good guys" deep down inside ourselves and also fear being "written off" if seen as we really are. If we're the least bit doubtful about the sterling quality of our character, we try even harder to look better, hoping that the doubt will go away.

In spite of all our efforts to build a good case for ourselves, we usually have no control over the events and circumstances that show us what we really are. Our character is truly tested when the pressure of life is turned on, and we can't always be prepared for those moments, can we? So we are frequently more shocked than anyone else when we don't turn out to be the good guys we thought we were.

Many people who have stopped caring still like to think of themselves as compassionate, concerned human beings. Many people who have run away from God still go to church every Sunday morning. They aren't being deliberately hypocritical, but they are leading two lives, and they don't realize how far apart the two are. Inside themselves these people have grown cold, bitter, resentful, and disillusioned, while outwardly they wear the garments of the Good Samaritan—until they see someone lying in a ditch. Then they find themselves passing by on the other side, muttering all kinds of excuses to themselves.

It's quite possible that Kitty Genovese's neighbors were shocked more by their own behavior than by the crime they witnessed—but they didn't want to talk about it.

They tried to dodge reporters, they were sullen during a court hearing of the case, and a year after the crime, when a mayoral candidate referred to the crime while making a campaign speech in the neighborhood, one of the witnesses said to another, "Oh, why does he have to bring that up?" We shouldn't be too hard on these people. If we had done the same thing, we probably wouldn't want to talk about it, either. And who knows how we'll meet our test when it comes?

We really ought to get to know who and what we are. It's been said that a good image is as precious as gold and as hard to find, but how can it be worth anything if it's only a front? Are we advertising a good guy who doesn't exist? And if he doesn't exist, who *is* that fellow inside us?

Maybe we ought to let somebody else worry about images while we concentrate on our character. If we're all right on the inside, the world will know it, sooner or later, because it will show through our feelings and our sensitivity to the feelings of others. The Apostle Paul was so right when he said that we are "flesh-and-blood letters." In fact, we might even go further and say that our lives are the only books by which people can "read" us.

If our lives don't measure up to our best intentions, we shouldn't blame anyone who points an accusing finger at us. People have to take stock of us according to what they see—they don't have the benefit of all the excuses we throw up in front of our own eyes.

Some people feel sorry for the underdog, but my heart often goes out to the villain in the story. I always wonder whether his behavior came as a surprise to him. Did he always think of himself as a man who wouldn't hurt a fly? Wasn't he like so many of us?

## 20. You Won't Get Far

Somewhere on a road along a sandy beach in southern France you can see one of the strangest landmarks in the world. I saw it one day when a friend was taking me to an airport, and his little boy suddenly interrupted our conversation with a squeal and a tug at my sleeve. "Look, Uncle Rube!" he said, "Did you see that?" I followed the line of his arm and saw a tall, circular, concrete stairway rising up out of the sand. It wasn't part of a house, a garage, or a building of any kind—it was just a stairway that was going nowhere.

What a peculiarly uneasy feeling that stairway gave me, and I turned my head to look back at it as we drove on. Why would anyone want to build such a structure? The sand around it looked as if it hadn't been disturbed for centuries, so I don't think the stairway had once been connected to something that had since fallen apart. Could it be that the builder was a man who wanted to get away from the world? And how did he feel when he found that he couldn't?

How hard we try to run from the things we don't like in our lives!—around and around we go, up to our winding staircases that go nowhere at all, and sooner or later we have to go right off the edge, or come back down the way we went up. Either way, we hit bottom—the very bottom we were trying to escape—and sometimes we're broken by the descent.

Lots of people don't like to keep their feet on the

ground. Ever since Adam, we haven't been satisfied with our living quarters on this earth, and we somehow got the idea that we belong somewhere in the uppermost layers of the universe. That may be quite true. Perhaps our preference for height is nothing more than the longing of our souls to be with God—but that will have to come in God's good time, and not ours.

We can't get far when we try to run from our reality. Trouble has a way of snapping at our heels when we make our mad dash for cover, and that's when we can really get hurt. People can get themselves killed by an overdose of escapism—hardly a day goes by when we don't read about someone whose life was a hectic shuffle between alcohol and barbiturates until the final terrible moment when the two closed in and choked out the life of their victim. Those people didn't want to die; they just wanted to "get away from it all," and unfortunately they succeeded too well! They didn't want to turn around and come down their "stairways to nowhere," and so they went over the edge.

This desire to escape does terrible things to our basic decency, and no wonder we are shocked by what we find in ourselves. A man who had been drinking heavily was driving home one evening when his car struck a pedestrian crossing the street. Even in his stupor the man realized he was at fault and he sped away from the motionless form in the road, not knowing whether he had hit a man, woman, or child—and not wanting to know. But life came after him in the form of the police, who traced his car and found him hiding in the attic of his house. There he was, huddled in a dark corner, trembling and weeping, wishing he could undo what he had done. And the worst part was yet to come—the person he had run down and left to die was his own son!

We shouldn't be too quick to point our finger at such a man. He wasn't very different from many of us who don't care for anything outside our own private lives. We mind our own business—we tell ourselves—and that's what everyone else should do, too! If we drive too fast or drink too much, that's our own business and nobody else's! We've sold ourselves a bill of goods in order to convince ourselves that we don't have to get involved with the things that are going on in the world; and while no one else may swallow our excuses, we often do. We forget that our lives still touch those of others, even though we may have turned away from them, and they are the ones we usually knock down in our hurry to run away.

For too many years we've been watching the soaring statistics of juvenile crime and delinquency, but we've told ourselves that our own kids were doing just fine. Somebody else's children were causing all the trouble, not ours. Now those statistics are telling us how wrong we were. They're telling us that those rebellious, angry, frightened young people are coming from *our* communities, from *our* churches, from *our* schools, and from *our* homes! Maybe you don't want to listen to the police officials who tell us that parents haven't been doing their duty toward their children, but you'll have to listen to some spokesmen for the armed forces because they see all kinds of kids from all kinds of backgrounds. And they tell us that our young people aren't in good shape— physically, morally, spiritually, or intellectually. The armed forces can't use a great many of them, and neither can the rest of the world, until we get in there and do the job we should have done many years ago.

Our young people reflect what has become of us, and it's hard for some of us to look at the picture. We'd rather not, and yet I don't see how we can avoid it. Our children are growing up, and their number is increasing, so that by 1985 two out of every five people in our country will be teen-agers! And those teen-agers will grow up into young men and women who must be given the reins of world leadership. That's right—ready or not, they're going to become responsible for your future, for mine, as well as their own, and that's when our involvement in their lives—or a lack of it—is really going to count. If we're selling them short now, we'll have to pay a stiff price for it later.

This old world is full of problems, and we just can't ignore them. If we do, the problems will only get worse. Some of us may think we don't want any part of them, but that only proves that we don't know ourselves very well. We human beings weren't meant to live always on the sidelines—we were meant for the rough-and-tumble action that takes place right in the middle of life too. That's where much of today's living is done, and why God put us in the world. When you get right down to it, we really don't have any choice but to live life at its best or its worst where we are.

## 21. "I Gotta Live, Don't I?"

It takes a heap of money to build a new church, or even to expand one, and probably most of us have had the experience of serving on a fund-raising committee. It's a tough job and it teaches you a great deal about people. Some of them really touch your heart when they reach deep down into their pockets, but some of them—well, it's a tough job!

We can appreciate the problems faced by a small congregation in a small community when they could no longer put off their need for a new church building. The old one was absolutely beyond repair, yet a new building meant that a lot of money had to be raised. The people in that town didn't have much money, and fund-raising wasn't going to be easy. The trustees of the church therefore decided to visit their more prosperous members first, so that their contributions might offer some encouragement to those who could afford to give only a small amount—that way, at least, they wouldn't feel that their goal couldn't ever be reached.

The first man on the visitation list was a farmer, the most well-to-do man in town, and he received the trustees with great courtesy. He listened patiently and with apparent interest while they explained the reason for their visit, and then he got up without a word and wrote out a check. The trustees looked at each other, not daring to break into the smiles they felt in their spirits, and each of them began to see in his mind a picture of the church they would build—how many Sunday-school classrooms they would need, and how many more pews! It was going to be a modest building, but it would gleam with glory to God.

Then the farmer gave them the check and when they looked at the amount of it, their faces fell. It was such a pitifully small contribution, much less than they would certainly get from the poorest member of the congregation! They were honest men, and brave ones, too, and they looked the farmer square in the eye as one of them said, "We really thought you would be able to do better than this."

The farmer was astonished. He stood up as straight as he could and snorted indignantly. "Well," he said, "I gotta live, don't I?"

One of the trustees—and it's my guess it was the youngest one—said, "Why?" and then they all left.

A few days later, the farmer rang the doorbell of the man who had asked him such a troubling question. He was a bit sheepish when the trustee opened the door but he went ahead with what he knew he must say. "I've been trying to answer your question," he said, "and it isn't easy. Why do I have to live? I guess I need a pretty big reason, don't I? And I'm not big enough, all by myself." He held out his hand and the trustee saw another check in it. "Yes, I can do much better," he said, "and maybe that's the beginning of a reason to live."

Everybody wants to find a reason for living, a meaning for life, and some of us look in the strangest places. We can't find a good enough reason anywhere within ourselves or our private lives—there just isn't enough material there to justify the miracle of our existence. We need to look for a reason outside ourselves, perhaps in the lives of other people, because when we mean something to others, we can begin to mean something to ourselves. It isn't enough to look at our reflection in the mirror and say, "Isn't it great that I'm here!" It's more important to ask, "What am I *doing* here?"

We put so much emphasis on our own lives and our own needs, yet the more attention we give to them, the more of a mess we make of them! Naturally, we have to take care of ourselves, but we shouldn't make a career of it. The rest of the world needs us badly—and strangely enough, that's exactly what we need. Psychiatrists tell us that one of the worst hungers in modern society is our need to be needed, and as we become more and more self-sufficient, this need gets less and less satisfaction.

Maybe this world could use more people who want to know rightly what's going on in other people's lives. We joke about the days when we had to share our telephone line with so many other families. We didn't like to have them listening in on our conversations or tying up the telephone when we wanted to use it, and we're so proud of the fact that even though there are more people in the world today, there are also more private telephone lines. But I question whether we can really call that "progress."

Eavesdropping used to be something no one wanted to be caught doing, but maybe it wasn't all bad. At least, if a heart broke, someone knew about it and possibly cared about it, too. These days, we're by circumstance much better behaved. We don't eavesdrop—not intentionally, anyway—and say we believe in "Live and Let Live." Unfortunately, this philosophy can turn out to be "Die and Let Die" when it goes too far.

New York City has been trying to deal with a serious problem of crime in its subways. Passengers have found themselves at the mercy of muggers, violent drunks brandishing weapons—anyone who wanted to terrorize people just had to get on board a train, and no one stopped him. People have been beaten, stabbed, shot, and robbed—in the presence of many other people who simply moved back a step to get out of danger—and there didn't seem to be any way to stop it. More police have been added to the subway force, but that won't offer a total solution as long as people don't care what happens to the fellow standing next to them.

One man didn't feel that his life was strictly his own affair. His name was Arthur Collins, and he was riding a subway, accompanied by his wife and infant, when a man came into the car and whipped out a gun. People screamed and huddled against the walls of the car, and that seemed to delight the gunman. He was quite plainly drunk and he staggered wildly from passenger to passenger, waving his gun in their faces and insulting them. Arthur Collins didn't like to see people treated that way—it made him cringe to see other human beings cringe—and he tried to wrestle the gun away from the man. But he was the only one who tried to do anything and he was no match for the terrorist. The gunman knocked Arthur Collins to the floor and shot him, killing him before the eyes of his wife and child. Then the train came to a stop at another station and no one tried to stop the killer as he escaped. Days later he was found by the police, but that didn't change the story for Arthur Collins.

I don't think anyone remembers the names of the other passengers in that subway—if they were ever reported—but Arthur Collins will stand for something in the minds of many people. I suppose that some of us will say that he was a fool to try to take a gun away from a drunken man, but many more of us will say that he was a very honest man, a complete realist. Arthur Collins seemed to know that none of us lives alone, that whatever happens to one of us happens to us all. He shared the fear that gripped the other passengers, and we must share the guilt for his death.

Yes, we've all "gotta live," don't we? And maybe it's time for us to get started doing exactly that—living! It's time for us to realize that we are the ones who suffer most when we stop caring; we are the ones we really leave behind when we try to run from our responsibility.

We're putting too much emphasis on the wrong kind of activity these days. We keep looking for things for our bodies to do and we're determined to keep ourselves physically fit—but we don't give our souls enough to do, and that's where much of our sickness is setting in. Our souls need plenty of exercise, and the best way to get them up and around is to learn from God to *care*!

## 22.  A Man-Sized Need

Have you ever been in a strange town or a city or a foreign country and run into someone from back home? Doesn't it make you feel warm and secure inside?

I remember walking through Tivoli Gardens in Copenhagen, Denmark, one summer, and it was one of the loveliest sights I will ever see. My wife and I had been away from home just long enough to be homesick. Somehow those colorful flowers seemed a bit less vivid to us than they really were. We found ourselves wondering what our family and friends were doing—and were they thinking of us?

Then we passed a restaurant and went in for a bite to eat. We sat down, feeling sadder every minute, and looked around for a waiter—and saw four familiar faces smiling at us from across the room. There was a man from Switzerland, one from Denmark, one from New York, and one from Minneapolis, all of them good friends of many years, and it took us exactly one split second to get to their table and join them. Gone was the homesickness—we weren't strangers any more, and when we went back to Tivoli Gardens to complete the tour, we could see the real color of the flowers. We had been with friends!

I travel a lot of the time, and I guess I'm luckier than most people who do, because I've been able to meet some friends and acquaintances almost everywhere I go. Once, I got off a plane in Paris and discovered that the man walking down the steps ahead of me was an old college chum, and we both expressed regret that we hadn't spotted each other at the beginning of the trip. Another time I was walking down the aisle of a department store in Rome when I met a woman who belonged to my church back home.

Yes, it's a very small world, but it seems so vast and empty when we're cut off from people—or when we cut ourselves off from them. We begin to realize how much we need each other when we have to leave our loved ones for a period of time, whether for business or vacation, but it helps to know that they're thinking of us while we're away. But are they? Some people have had the misfortune to discover that the old saying, "Out of sight, out of mind," can be painfully true.

Most of us were not only angered but confused when we were forced to add the word "brainwashing" to our vocabulary. It's an ugly word and its definition is even worse, but we had to start learning it during the Korean conflict when a few Americans who were taken prisoner by the Communists decided that they didn't want to come home when the fighting was over. They preferred the Communist way of life and they broadcast their preference "loud and clear" to all the world. There really weren't many of these men, but the fact that there was even one was distressing to many Americans, including me. Our country seems to offer so much to a man—how could it ever repulse anyone?

Well, I heard at least part of an answer to this question when I attended a conference in Pensacola, Florida, at that time, and one of the speakers was a Navy man who had had a great deal of experience with the problems that came out of the Korean fighting. He had spoken to some of the men whose brains had been "washed" by the Communists, and he found that they were a very bitter group of men. They had been through some rough fighting during the conflict, and they had been good soldiers, but all of a sudden they began to get the idea that the people back home really didn't care what became of them. They read some newspapers from the States and they saw that the hostilities in Korea weren't taking up much space on the pages. Life seemed to be going on as usual back home, and this came as a stunning blow to some of the men who shivered in the cold night, high up on a bleak mountain where they might be cut down by a sniper's bullet or overrun by a fiendishly shrieking horde of men wearing cheaply-made padded uniforms and blowing bugles as they charged. Perhaps they thought of their families back home, sitting down to an evening of television after a big dinner, and flipping the dial until they came to something comical so they wouldn't have to think of all the terrible things going on in the world.

This does not excuse the strange behavior of men who would turn against their country—and in this case, even their God—but it does give us a clue to it. While it does not explain exactly what happened, it may offer us enough insight so that we can see to it that it doesn't have to happen ever again.

People shouldn't have to go through life by themselves. They shouldn't ever feel that no one cares about them. But they do, and they don't have to go through armed battle to become embittered about it. In fact, I think all of us have felt abandoned at some time or another—and we were glad if we discovered that we were just "imagining" it. Who knows how we might have behaved if we had found it to be true!

I remember an elderly clergyman I knew many years ago, a man who thought he had been born too soon. His name was Ole and he marveled at all the things a young, modern minister could learn these days. Why, a minister could supposedly be all kinds of things in one!—a preacher, teacher, a marriage counselor, a youth director, a psychologist, a sociologist, an administrator, an economist, a political scientist, a fund-raiser, a vocational and recreational guidance counselor! Ole thought he was too old to be any of these things—he was a plain minister, and to his mind not such a good one! But he did have one specialty—he could get through to people, young and old alike.

One night Ole received a call from a funeral director, who told him that one of his parishioners had died. The family of the dead man were so thunderstruck by his sudden death that they couldn't even call their pastor, and the funeral director had been sensitive to their need for him.

It was very late, but Ole went to the hall closet, got out his heavy overcoat, put it on, and laboriously buttoned every single button. He seemed to be taking his time, but he knew exactly what he was doing. Death moves fast as it snatches up our loved ones and breaks our lives into pieces—but it takes time to put those pieces back together again, as best we can, and that can't be done in a hurry. Ole went out to the garage, got his car out, and drove off.

When he arrived at the home of the grieving family, he found the mother and children near hysteria. They had been a close, loving family, and the father had been a fairly young man whose death was completely unexpected. Wonderful old Ole stood in the doorway, saying nothing, unbuttoning his overcoat. He hadn't ever been given a course in "What to Do for the Bereaved" because schools didn't teach such things when he was a theological student, and so he had to rely on the things he had learned from God, from Christ, from the Bible, and from his long experience of caring for people.

Ole rubbed his chin slowly and methodically as he looked from the mother to one child, and then to another and another. "Ja, Ja, Ja," he muttered to himself in the thick Norwegian accent he had never lost. Then he walked over to the weeping woman and touched her shoulder. "Ja, Ja, Ja," he said, softly. And then as he went to each child and did the same thing, he seemed to be lifting some of the burden from each of them and taking it upon his own once-massive shoulders.

Suddenly he turned to the mother and said, "Now—put on the coffee pot!" It was almost a command, although a gentle one, and the woman seemed to gather her strength to stand up, move to the stove, pick up the percolator—and at the same time pick up one of the broken threads of her life.

Ole didn't know a thing from psychology books, but he knew people and he could sense the deep need all of us have. He could find the common denominator—in this case, an old coffee pot—that could draw people back into a comfortable relationship with each other. When he had arrived at that home, each member of the family had been locked in a closet of grief, completely cut off from the others. Ole unlocked the doors of those closets and brought the family back into a unit where they could help each other in their sorrow.

The human race forms a kind of unit, too, and each of us has a place in it. We may feel so insignificant when we're all by ourselves, but put us in our proper places with right spirits and we can suddenly take on a great importance. We will find that we've been missed by all the people who needed us so badly!

## 23. Guidance Takes Guts

Wouldn't it be nice if we could foretell the future?
Maybe not. We might not like what we see there.

Two noted criminologists recently made an exhaustive
study of delinquent and so-called normal young people
to find out whether delinquency could be predicted.
According to them, it could. Some well-developed and
troublesome characteristics found in the delinquents
were already detectable in some of the normal youngsters,
and on the basis of these similarities the scientists could
point to a particular boy and say—with 85 to 90 percent
certainty—that he would eventually be a delinquent.

That's disturbing, especially to parents who care—and
most of us do. But we don't always care in the right ways,
and this is how we can do a lot of harm without realizing
it.

On the basis of their study, the criminologists drew
some interesting conclusions that can help all of us. They
found that the youngsters who seemed to be doing well
—those who appeared likely to avoid serious trouble as
they grew into maturity—were those who came from
homes in which among other things there had been
adequate supervision. In other words, Mom and Dad,
or someone with authority, always knew where Johnny
was—and Johnny didn't go where they didn't want
him to be. These children had had a set of rules to guide
them in their growing years, and not only did they know
where they were but to whom they belonged.

I suppose this might be considered a rather old-fashioned kind of upbringing that is fast leaving the scene of the modern home, but I wish we'd give it a chance to make a comeback. Many of us like to think of ourselves as progressive parents who want to give our children every possible chance to develop their personalities, but we may be overlooking a more important kind of progressive education—the progressive understanding of the meaning of love. This is really what our children need, and this is what they're trying to tell us when they kick up their heels with such dangerous consequences to themselves.

If we let our children express themselves by doing whatever they please, we're being permissive but not necessarily loving. Love cares about the quality of the personality in a child; it isn't willing to take any old characteristics that come out of a child and just settle for them. Love wants a child to grow up into a fine, responsible, caring, loving person, and it doesn't shrink from the patient, exhaustive molding such an upbringing requires.

Our kids want to know that we claim them. I'm sure they enjoy those records and sports cars and snappy clothes we give them, whenever we can afford them; but if it came to a decision, I think our kids would choose our love rather than our merchandise any day.

Who was your favorite teacher, the one from whom you learned the most? Was he or she the most brilliant, the most eloquent, or the best-looking teacher you had? Probably not. Most of us will never forget our favorite teacher—and in most cases it was a woman—and chances are she was the teacher who loved her students the most. She was probably a pretty good disciplinarian, too.

Teachers find it fairly hard to love their classes today

because so many of their students come from homes where they have never had to submit to any authority. Mom and Dad are too busy trying to be buddies to their children, and they usually end up as their puppets. They learn to talk as the young people do, they even dress like them and sing their songs—but they never understand them. They seem to forget that a child without guidance doesn't know which way to turn. Responsibility only confuses him, and then he gets angry—and we get angry. "Blame it on this one, blame it on that one!" we cry, but that won't help a child who's hurt.

How many times I've seen an annoyed expression on a parent's face at the mention of "discipline"! It's a problem that really bothers them, and the worst part of it is this matter of where to draw the line, "It's not so hard for me to make up my mind about what's good or bad for Bob," one mother told me, "but I have trouble with the competition—with the parents of Bob's friends. What should I do when I say 'no' to something Bob wants to do, and he looks at me and says, 'Well, so-and-so's mother is letting so-and-so do it, so why can't I?' What do I do under that kind of pressure?"

"Hold the line," I said. "Who's responsible for Bob?— you or his friend's mother?"

She sighed and made a face. "That's going to take guts," she said, and I fully agreed with her.

It does take guts to bring up our children. If we care about the things they are doing, saying, thinking, feeling, we have to get involved in their lives so that we can learn what is going on. This means we may have to withstand their disapproval now and then, and it means that we have to show our children that discipline, or a set of rules, is a form of love. When they begin to understand this, they probably won't want us to be their buddies, but they'll be happy and relieved to have us as parents—parents who care. "Train up a child in the way he should go: and when he is old he will not depart from it" (PROVERBS 22:6, KJV).

## 24. Business Means People

Some of us may not look upon machines with much kindness, especially when we're afraid that they may throw us out of work, but they've already done human beings a big favor. They've taught the men who manage business that they can't treat people like machines.

You can't push a button and turn off your problems for the seven or eight hours you spend on your job, and this is something your boss is beginning to understand. People often take their troubles to work with them, and that can be dangerous—it can cause some pretty terrible accidents.

Some businessmen have learned a valuable lesson. They know now that when they don't care about people as people it can cost them money. They realize that their responsibility to their employees can go far beyond a salary and fringe benefits. It can include the entire well-being of the employees—their physical, mental, and spiritual health. I suppose that's why some companies now have chaplains on their staffs.

I met two of these chaplains one day, and when they described the nature of their work I must admit that I felt like patting the industrial world on the back. In one sense, at least, they are far ahead of many—they're caring more, not less, about their most valuable asset, people.

I suppose that some people might say, "What in the world can a chaplain do in the business world?" but I don't think they ever find themselves with time on their hands. What does a man do when he has trouble making ends meet? Does he sit home and brood about it? He does not! He has to get up in the morning—the same as the rest of us—and go to work. And what about the woman who still grieves over the death of her mother? She has to go to work, too, even though her heart is still in mourning. The fellow who works next to you may be scared to death inside himself, but he still has to put in a day's work.

Don't you think some of these people would like to talk to someone? Haven't you ever felt that way? Haven't you ever wanted to put your head down on your desk and cry those tears you're trying to hold back until quitting time? But people might not understand. Your boss might think you're cracking up and change his mind about giving you that promotion—he might even think about replacing you! No, you've got to show everybody that you're steady, dependable, responsible, and completely free of troubles! 'Til the very last moment, 'til the time when you break apart in a million unmendable pieces, you'll carry on with that stiff-upper-lip routine, won't you?

This has been the fate of too many people who were trying to make their way in the world, and, finally, the men who run the nation's businesses began to see that it was costing them more than money—it was depriving them of their best workers. And they realized, too, that they could add something, both for greater effectiveness in work as well as an expression of caring. Naturally, every company wants to feel that its employees are loyal to it, but loyalty has to come from a partnership that works both ways. Both employee and management need to feel that they get a return on the investment of time,

99

education and training, judgment, intelligence, patience, hopes, initiative, skill, determination, ambition, and deep concern. Both want to know that the other cares about what goes on inside him!

The employee wants more than the security of a guaranteed income and old-age benefits—he needs the security of knowing that his company will stand by him when the going gets rough. He wants to know that he can go and talk to someone—maybe a chaplain, if there is one, but more likely a personnel manager or a department head who doesn't feel that people in crises should keep their troubles to themselves. People get a lot of help out of talking through their worries, but they need someone somewhere who will listen to them—and for no other reason than that they care!

If the business world has begun to realize that people need more than financial security (they need to be persons), where does that leave the rest of us? We're supposed to have big, warm hearts, yet when we don't pay any attention to a cry for help from the fellow who works right alongside us, aren't we really behaving like machines?

## 25. Rebellion Within Reason

"When do these students ever find time to attend their classes?" muttered a man who sat next to me on a plane. He was reading a news report of a student "protest"—something you can find every day in your own newspapers—and it obviously made him angry. "Where do they do their studying? Out in the streets?" he asked, and since he wasn't speaking to me directly, I didn't try to answer. I wouldn't have known what to say, anyway.

Probably most of us are puzzled by the things that are happening on our campuses, and we can sympathize with university officials and the embarrassment they must feel when their students tell them how to do their job. We wouldn't like to be in their shoes—but we really are! Our young people are telling their college administrators the same thing they're telling us—they don't like the conditions of the world we're leaving to them!

In this sense, we should be able to sympathize with these students, too, because we once thought we could run the world better than our elders—remember? Oh, we didn't run around waving posters and chanting slogans and making quite as much noise as our present generation of protesters, but we did some fairly outlandish things. And we did them because we had a cause, because we wanted to right something we thought was wrong.

Our young people have very strong feelings about their causes, too, and if they make a bigger commotion about them, perhaps that is the only way they can get this busy, noisy world's attention. It might also be that theirs is simply another generation with its own way of expressing itself.

Rebellion somehow seems to be a natural part of youth —just as our alarm over any form of rebellion is probably a natural part of our older age. But I don't think we're completely wrong when we question some of the outlets rebellion is seeking these days.

There are two kinds of rebellion, the positive and the negative, and we can find examples of either kind any day in the week. People who rebel in a positive way have something to contribute to the world, and they can't always make their contribution through the traditional channels. Sometimes they think they have to break a few rules and regulations, or just old patterns, in order to "get through" to us.

Frank Lloyd Wright, the architect, was one of these people who broke with the old patterns. I remember seeing him get off a train many years ago, and at a glance you could tell that he was a unique individual. Even the way he wore his white hair—long and flowing—was different, and while it might have looked idiotic on someone else, it seemed to suit him. Thomas Alva Edison was another positive type of rebel who simply could not accept the possibility that a man's mind had to submit to limitations. He didn't believe that the world had progressed as far as it could—he *had to* make some more improvements.

The world owes much to a great many others who rebelled—but within reason. Their cause was the betterment of the world, and on this they spent their imagination, their dreams, their prayers, and often their lives.

The other kind of rebellion, the negative kind, hasn't

produced the kind of names we remember with gratitude, although we must admit that they have often awakened us to some grim realities of life. But negative rebels have a talent for needling us, because they tell us what is wrong with the world without offering any way to improve it. They break rules, too, but sometimes they don't stop to make a distinction between a good rule and a bad one, and we may be right in suspecting them of breaking them for the sheer fun of it. These rebels seem to have no contribution to make to this world after they've torn it down—they have no hope for the betterment of life, and very little regard for anyone's feelings. But perhaps with some it is an indefinable rebellion against adults' hypocrisy and false values.

What kind of a rebel is your child? What kind will he grow up to be? You might as well face the fact that he's going to protest against something—if he doesn't, you may have something to worry about—and you will have a lot to do with the way he does it. Is he the kind who desperately needs attention? Does he attach himself to any old movement simply because it gives him a chance to let off steam? Is he a rebel for the sake of rebellion itself? If he is, then he needs your earnest care, because he's fast approaching the point where he is incapable of caring about anything—this child is out to tear the world apart, and he'll probably let it stay that way!

A rebel within reason and with high purpose can make a mighty noise, too, but he may also be a quiet protester, when he sees that this is the best way to further his cause. You see, he's not trying to get something for himself out of all the fuss he makes—he's trying to give something to a world about which he is deeply concerned.

I'm thinking now of the most gentle, forceful, soft-spoken, hard-talking Rebel mankind has ever known—

Jesus Christ, who certainly could have merely criticized and shattered, if that had been His aim. But it wasn't. He found much that was wrong with our life here on earth and with us. He didn't hesitate to point a finger at it or us, but He didn't leave us with despair in our hearts. He gave us hope by showing us a better Way and a better Life. And He Himself was and is These.

## 26. Plenty of Strings Attached

One of the reasons we can't do much about the weather is that we don't look at it realistically. In the cold of winter, as we're scurrying across windy streets and snuggling as deep into our overcoats as we can possibly squeeze, we find ourselves remembering the wonderful days of summer. We recall the picnics, the longer hours of daylight, the hours spent swimming, golfing, fishing, or just loafing, and we wonder why life can't always be that way.

Of course, we're forgetting how we really felt last summer when we were sweltering in a heat wave, complaining about the humidity that tired us out before we got through half the day. We're forgetting the nights when we tossed and turned, trying to forget the heat and fall asleep, and with no success. Another morning, another soaring temperature, and—oh, won't we be glad when those cold, crispy winter days get here!

We're all the same—we keep the memories we like and throw the others away, which means that some of our experiences don't make any impression on us at all.

I was thinking about the weather one day when I was in Pittsburgh during a snowfall that gave the city a very hard time. My radio was turned on, and I thought I was hearing things when the announcer began to urge people to stay at home, stay at their jobs—wherever they were, they were to stay put! No, it was quite true, and I had heard correctly, as I discovered when the announcer repeated his message. I knew it had been snowing a short time, but it hadn't looked like a blizzard, by any means, yet when I went to the window I was astonished to see that traffic in the streets was completely snarled up. Horns were blowing, policemen were using their whistles in an effort to get things moving, drivers were shouting at each other, and people on foot were darting in between the cars and climbing over bumpers when there wasn't enough space for them to get through. Still, I couldn't see much snow on the ground, and very little was falling from the sky.

I was used to real winters back in Minneapolis, Minnesota, and all the fuss people were making over such a little bit of snow amused me. Why, back in Minnesota, an inch and a half of snow wouldn't even slow us down, and we could even take twelve inches in our stride! Then I looked out the window again and I began to understand what was causing all the trouble.

Pittsburgh is a city built on hills, and its roadways wind through them, around them, or over them, which means that they have to make a lot of turns. The traffic simply can't roll right straight through, as it does in some parts of the country. So even a little bit of snow can be a problem, especially when a car or a truck gets stuck while making a turn around one of those bends in the road. One stall, one breakdown, one car that skids and spins around, can back up traffic throughout the city and create a crisis.

Isn't this similar to some of the events that happen in the lives of people? Isn't it true that we can get caught up in a traffic jam not of our own making? Even though we can't see very far ahead, our way may be temporarily barred by a human life that suddenly jack-knifed while going around a bend.

What are we supposed to do when something like this happens? Do we sit still and wait until the road is cleared? Do we get out and walk back to our homes, swearing that we'll never use that road again?

What's our attitude toward these people who stall or break down right smack in the middle of our path? Some of us may not remember having such an experience in our own lives, and we may be somewhat impatient when we're held up by someone else's flat tire. We may ask ourselves why others can't barrel through life as smoothly as we do. We solve our own problems—why can't they? And if they can't solve them, why don't they get off the main roads of life?

But aren't we forgetting something? Aren't we forgetting those times when we had to go through some winding roads that weren't even paved? and haven't we lived through some rough storms, too? Are we forgetting how bad they really were? Are we remembering only the cool rain that splashed on our faces, and forgetting the ground that became a dangerous slick of mud under our feet?

Maybe some people laughed when they heard that Pittsburgh was tied up by an inch and a half of snow, but I didn't—at least, not when I realized how Pittsburgh was built. Some of us may laugh—and even sneer—when we see people all tied up with problems that seem quite insignificant. The trouble is that we can't see more than a short stretch of their lives from where we stand. We can't see that a life may be stalled by greater problems —or by the lives of others—somewhere up ahead.

When we allow ourselves to care about people and the things that upset their lives, we find that we can see so much better. We can take a good look at our own lives and see that they weren't all sweetness and light, after all—we've had our share of some pretty hard times, and we got through them because someone came by and gave us a hand.

Everybody's trying to get away from traffic these days, but I don't think they'll succeed permanently, because traffic is a vital part of life. It follows people wherever they go, and the angrier they get about it, the worse the traffic jam becomes. We've been trying to get through life on secondary roads for a long time now, and we're finding that they're not much better than a detour. We simply have to get back on the main roads if we want to go anywhere, and that means that we'll have to make our way through the heavy traffic.

The next time we're held up by another life that's in trouble, maybe we ought to try something other than blowing a horn or blowing our tops. As long as we think only of ourselves, we aren't being very practical because we won't be able to move until that breakdown up ahead is repaired.

Couldn't we try getting out of our car, and walking ahead to where the trouble is, and lending a hand? Isn't that the very best way to get where we want to go?

## 27. "Bridges Have to Be"

Bridges take a long time to build, but they're among man's proudest achievements. Each one means that somewhere, sometime, a man got tired of staring at a body of water and decided to get across to the other side, to connect himself with something else.

Not long ago, New York celebrated the opening of the Verrazano Narrows Bridge, connecting Brooklyn with Staten Island, one of the last country spots in the metropolitan area, and it was quite an event. The bridge is the longest in the world and it deserves all the cheers and speeches and band music it got on opening day.

Not everybody was happy about the bridge. Some of the men who worked on it had been killed in accidents during the many months of its construction, and we can understand why their wives and children probably wished no one had ever thought of building that bridge. Then there were some residents on Staten Island who knew that the bridge would bring more people out from the city, and that would change their rural way of life. They were perfectly content with the old Staten Island Ferry that used to take them back and forth to the city—it may have been an old-fashioned means of transportation, but so was its price of a nickel a ride!

But most people were delighted to see the bridge completed. It meant that people who owned land on Staten Island would get a good price for it if they wanted to sell it—and they wouldn't have to wait long for buyers because now that the bridge was open, commuting was a snap, and lots of people would be looking for houses on the Island. It meant, too, that Staten Island was no longer a distant spot of land out there in the harbor—now everybody could see that it was definitely a part of the city.

Of course, some people like to live in isolated parts of the world, and if they can't manage to get to them, they somehow go on living as if they were on an island out in the middle of nowhere. You might live next door to someone like that—someone you've seen almost every day for years, but who looks the other way when you're trying to catch his eye and say "hello." In fact, you may be an islander yourself—but let's hope not!

A constantly isolated life is not for you, for me, or for any other human being, no matter how much we may think we like it that way. As one man on Staten Island said, when he was asked if he felt bitter about the bridge —"Bridges have to be, that's all." At least he knew when life was catching up with him.

City people try to live in isolation, but they usually call it "privacy," and maybe they have a good excuse for it because they have to live so close to each other. But the spiritual distance they put between themselves and the tenant in the apartment upstairs is more than ceiling high! Herb Caen, a San Francisco columnist, remarked about this back in 1962 when the San Francisco Giants and the Los Angeles Dodgers were in a baseball play-off to determine which team would win the pennant and go on to play in the World Series. It seems that the people in San Francisco, like most people in big cities, don't get very friendly with each other—at least they didn't until baseball brought them together in one big wave of excitement. Suddenly everybody had something to say, and they said it to the man sitting next to them on the trolley, to the next-door neighbor they met in the hall, to the waitress in the restaurant, the elevator operator—anybody!—and the city suddenly knew the warmth of human communication. In a matter of hours, bridges had been built, connecting thousands of lives, and not all those bridges disappeared when the ball games were over.

I had a chance to help in the building of a bridge between two people when I was a guest aboard an aircraft carrier anchored off the coast of California one recent summer. I was having an exciting time exploring the great ship—thanks to the commanding officer, who was an old friend of mine—but when I stopped indulging myself for a moment I noticed the "green" young aide to the commanding officer. He was obviously very nervous in the presence of his superior, and I assumed—correctly, as it turned out—that he hadn't been aboard for long. He stood by us rigidly, and he jumped so noticeably when the captain spoke to him that he deserved and got every ounce of my sympathy.

When the young officer joined us for dinner, I had a better chance to speak to him and I asked him what his hometown was. "Glen Ellyn, Illinois," he said, most formally and without turning his eyes away from the wall in front of him. I asked some more questions and learned that the young man had lived for a long time near the Loop in Chicago, and also near a lake outside Minneapolis, where his grandparents had lived for many years, and that his father was in the appliance business.

"That's interesting," I said, "and I rather think I can guess some of the names on your family tree." This brought his head around in a hurry. "Wasn't your dad named Bob?" I asked, completely startling him. "Yes!" he said.

"And your mother—your mother is Magna. Then there's

111

your Uncle Clarence, your Aunt Dorothy—" and on and on I went, through both sets of grandparents, while the young man relaxed into a huge grin. We were connected by a bridge of people we had both known.

Then I said—turning toward my friend the commanding officer, who had been listening to the last part of our conversation—"I'd like you to meet a college classmate of your dad's, young man—your captain!" Both men were surprised, not only because they had roots in the same school, but because they hadn't already discovered it.

When I left the ship the next day I could see that the relationship between captain and aide had changed enormously. Oh, there was no doubt which officer was which, and one was an experienced man of the sea while the other was still a youngster in the Navy, but there was a bridge of friendship between them, and it made all the difference in the world. The captain was no longer isolated by his authority, and the tense young aide was no longer stranded on an island of inexperience or fear.

Yes, bridges have to be, and we can't hold out forever in our isolated lives. Our supplies are running low, and we need the nourishment that comes from other lives reaching out to us. The trouble is that we have been trying to "go it alone" for so long that we've forgotten how related we all are. That's right—we're all made in the image of Almighty God Himself, and we'll never know real comfort in this world until we realize that we have a tremendous family tree.

But how do we get in touch with our relatives again? And how will they recognize us after such a long time of not caring? How can those bridges be built? No, we can't do it by ourselves—we need a Master Builder. We need God's very Son to bring us back into touch with each other again.

## 28. The Man Who Cared

God sent a message to us almost two-thousand years ago when a Child was born in a Bethlehem manger. It was a very simple message—"I love you."

Now, people in those days weren't any different from us, and many of them thought that the Child, grown into manhood, couldn't possibly be the Son of God, as He said He was. Why, God would send His Son to earth in a spectacular burst of stars, or something like that, and His Child would have the best of everything—people would bow before Him wherever He went, and if they were lucky, He might cast His eyes upon them! But this—this Carpenter Person—would never do as the Son of God!

And so, this Man "who wouldn't do" went about His Father's business and changed the entire world! He was not only the perfect Son of God, but a perfect Messenger as well. Divine as He was, He also knew what it was to walk the dusty earth, to feel its dryness in His throat, to seek the coolness of shade under a desert tree, and to cry to His God in His human anguish. He, whose Father made us, taught us the meaning of humility as He traveled the countryside, walked the city streets, talked to people, healed them, listened to their sorrows —*and wept*. But the message was not yet spelled out, and His journey was not yet over. It ended up ahead, on a hill called Calvary, where He was crucified by the people for whom His message of love was intended— then moved on to Resurrection victory.

Some people have strange notions about the nature of God. Some of them imagine Him to be a kind of automaton who does nothing but punish and condemn, punish and condemn, but these people have clearly never known the God who is Love. Then there are those who think of God as a rather small, vague something-or-other, way off in the distance—a puny creature compared to their own great big selves! And then there are those who lift up their hearts in thankful prayer because the great Almighty God can look with love upon each and every little, tiny, insignificant human being! Regardless of how we think of God—humbly or arrogantly—He knows only one way to think of us, and that is lovingly.

In a sense, God has addressed Himself to us through His creation of the world, and of man himself, and He has signed His message "Sincerely Yours." But what kind of letter does He usually receive from us? Isn't it usually a demand?—"Gimme, gimme! More and more!" And how do we sign our little notes?—"Sincerely *Mine!*" We're very poor letter-writers, aren't we? Many of us don't even bother to write any more.

But God knows who and what we are, and He knows that most of us have to be shown, not told, what Love is all about, and so He arranged to have His message delivered in Person—in the Person of Jesus Christ, His Son!

Now, this must have been a very important message, and indeed it was. God through Christ was saying, "I love you, My creation; I want you to know My love, to be won to it, to be reborn in it. Because I love you in spite of yourselves, I want you to know the experience of being caught up—not only within My will and purpose, but to live within the circle of My reclaiming power. I want you to know the wholeness of your personality by discovering the joy of being 'at oneness' with Me!" And the message was signed—in the agony and blood of His Son upon the cross—"Sincerely Yours."

Do we really have the right to say we've had our fill of the human race? Can we turn a deaf ear to the cry of human need and convince ourselves that our own skins are the only ones that really matter? I don't think so. Somehow, when we turn away from our brother-beings, we turn away from our own souls as well—and there's an obvious reason for this. We were made in the image of our Father, and our souls were claimed by the love of His Blessed Son, and when we try to live without loving, we are, in a sense, going against His creative intention—we're living against the grain of refashioned souls, and we just can't get away with it comfortably.

Until we turn around and find our way back to the God who reaches out to us, we'll never be completely happy. We'll always be nagged by the memory of the days when we could have cared about the world, about the people who try to live in it—however imperfectly—and about our relationship with the God who created it. It seems like a long journey, but Christ comes to meet us. Perhaps we can travel more quickly if we reach out and take the hand of a brother along the way. And if that brother pulls back, slowing us down—and if he hurts us and causes us to stumble—we'll just have to do as God has done before us—*forgive him,* and say of our lives addressed to God and others, "Sincerely Yours."

## 29. Your Giveaway Program

This is a great age for prizes, for bonuses, two-for-the price-of-one, and free gift offers. We're giving all kinds of things to each other, and we're almost looking for excuses to exchange presents. But when the chips are down, we find that material things don't really mean that much.

It didn't mean anything to the people in Anchorage, Alaska, when a tremendous earthquake swallowed up most of their homes in the spring of 1963. You can imagine the anguish and horror people felt as they saw the result of years of labor breaking up beneath their feet—and yet, in that dreadful moment, everyone knew that the one thing they really wanted to save was life itself. Everything else could be replaced someday—but not life.

Lowell Thomas, Jr., his wife, and two children had lived in Anchorage for some time before the earthquake, and they were accustomed to interesting experiences, having shared many adventures with Lowell Thomas, Sr., in his travels throughout the world. But this was surely more than excitement—it was soul-shaking. As Kay Prior Thomas described it, their house was on the edge of a cliff, which began to shift and rumble when tremors first began to disturb the earth, and within a few minutes, they found themselves stranded on a great cold slab of earth surrounded by ever-widening cracks that seemed to have no bottom. Down, down, down, the piece of earth slipped, carrying the Thomases toward the Bay at the bottom of the cliff, and then—miraculously, they thought —it stopped and lodged in the rubble, and the Thomases gratefully began the long climb back up the cliff.

The disaster occurred on Good Friday and it left the townspeople stunned and frightened. They didn't know where to begin to rebuild, and there were alarming rumors of more quakes to come—what were they going to do? Some of them knew where to look for the answer, because the churches were filled on Easter morning, two days later.

When the Thomases went to church, the air was frosty and cold, and people's breath came in quick, white puffs, but they sang as never before in all their lives. Most of us find that Easter gives us a reason to be happy, but the people of Anchorage apparently felt they had been doubly blessed. When the Thomases were leaving the church they stopped to read two lists posted on the bulletin board in the vestibule—one was a list of "haves," useful items people were ready to give away or share with those who might need them, and the other was a list of "have-nots," items people needed. Interestingly, the "have-not" list was very small, but the "have" list filled the page! In spite of all they had lost, most people felt they had so much they could afford to give—*they had life!*

No matter how broke or how well off we are, each of us has a lot to give away, and the sooner we begin doing it, the better we are going to feel. We've been trying to fool ourselves into thinking that we could be happy if we kept ourselves to ourselves, and deep in our souls I think we really know better.

Some of us have been very generous in giving material gifts, and perhaps we're beginning to see that we don't get anything meaningful in return. We give someone a beautiful scarf or a handsome sweater, and what happens?

They give us a scarf or a pair of slippers—and maybe they're beautiful, too, but they just don't seem to say anything. Anyone can go out and buy that kind of a gift as long as he can pay the price—it's a totally material transaction that touches the hands and not the heart.

There is another kind of gift, one that is not material, and yet it has the deepest meaning. It is the gift of ourselves, and it is given by caring, by loving, by becoming involved in the lives of others to the point where we can actually share their sorrows as well as their joys.

I stopped in to see an elderly woman I have known for many years, and asked her how she was getting along. "Just wonderfully," she said; "There is a fine gentleman who lives next door, and every day he stops in to see how I am." That fine gentleman had given a great gift that cost him a few minutes of his time and a little bit of care— and what a difference it made in one human life!

It's amazing, but we stand to gain something from giving ourselves away—because there's a tremendous satisfaction in allowing ourselves to belong to somebody else. We no longer feel so impatient with the world because we can understand it better. Caring makes us sensitive to the feelings of others, and when we realize that things might not be going too well for them, perhaps we can do something about it—thereby lighting up our own lives as well as theirs.

As Emerson observed, rings and jewels are not gifts but the excuses for gifts, and the cards you enclose with them might as well not be signed if there is nothing of yourself in such presents. Love is the only gift that can express something of yourself, the only gift that is worthy of bearing the name of the giver.

## 30.  Sure, It'll Cost You!

Maybe some folks can say that "life is just a bowl of cherries," but I'm sure most of us have had a somewhat different experience. We've probably found a few sour apples in among the cherries because, quite simply, that's the way life is.

It's the same with people—you'll find good and bad—but if you want to have any kind of a warm relationship with them, you have to be willing to get hurt now and then. We all do our share of the hurting, too, because that's the way people are.

Many years ago, a little girl was trying to finish a bowl of oatmeal—or mush, as we used to all it—and she was having a very difficult time because she absolutely hated it. But she was a brave little girl and swallowed mouthful after mouthful until her bowl was empty, and then she pushed her plate away from her and said, "You know, God, I can hardly stand that stuff!"

That's the way you'll feel about life's disappointments, its aches and pains, if you're the kind of person who can take them in stride. You won't like them, and you'll wince every time you get hurt, but you'll realize that you shouldn't try to avoid them—there's always something you can learn from them!

But some people are terribly afraid of getting hurt and they allow this fear to keep them from living life abundantly. They allow it to keep them from knowing people, from becoming interested in their lives and sharing in their feelings, and life away from people is pretty

119

colorless. It may not be painful, in the ordinary sense of the word, but it isn't happy, either—it's just dull, endlessly dull.

People are tough critters, and they can take a lot more pain than they realize. We always tend to think of pain as a dead-end experience, but it's really a dark valley through which we must occasionally pass—and it can lead us to some wonderfully interesting places.

John Glenn, the first American to orbit the earth, had literally been on top of the world, and so he was not prepared for the "valley experience" that he was to pass through not long after he became a celebrated national hero. He was looking forward to a thrilling future and was even planning to run for Congress when he had the kind of accident that most of us consider a joke—he slipped in his bathroom, injured himself, and was left with severe dizzy spells. That meant the end of his campaign plans, and the end of most of his many activities, because John Glenn had to spend some time off his feet. Then his wife became ill, then his father and his mother, too, and on top of the illnesses came financial setbacks. Would the blows ever stop?

Surely this man, who had braved the unknown frontiers of outer space, was confused to find himself being battered mercilessly by the ways of life, and yet he was able to find a strength greater than that which gave him the courage to soar in a rocket. "There is a luxury in a thing like this being forced upon you," he said. "You stop to see where you are going. You pick up all the pieces and start in the direction you feel is best."

John Glenn is a man who prays to God, a man who asks God which way he should go in life. Perhaps this is why life's pain did not become a dead-end experience for him.

Alvin C. York was another man who was well acquainted with pain, and in many different forms. He used to be a cussin', hard-drinkin' Cumberland Mountain troublemaker until, as Alvin put it, the Lord knocked him off his horse with a thunderbolt. And it must have been a thunderbolt of love, because God surely changed Alvin York. He had once been a menace with a rifle, but that became a thing of the past. Alvin put his gun away, because he didn't believe in killing any more—and he didn't believe in war, either, but when World War I came along he wasn't excused from military service. Then, one day, when his fellow soldiers were dropping all around him under the machine-gun fire of the enemy in a French forest, Alvin York had to make a decision that must have caused him great pain. He didn't want to use his gun, but he knew what he had to do. He lifted his rifle to his shoulder, took aim with an eye that had never lost its ability to sight a target, and when the battle was over, Sergeant York was a hero, a man who had killed, wounded, and captured an amazing number of German soldiers. Even this strange notoriety must have hurt him, because Alvin York had learned to love his fellowmen.

I suppose Sergeant York just wanted to go home to the Tennessee hills and rest his weary soul, but the world wouldn't let go of his coattails. It carried him on its shoulders, paraded him under clouds of ticker tape and scrap paper in its big cities, and hounded him to become a movie star, a super salesman, a big wheel; and when Alvin turned away, saying, "My uniform is not for sale," the world got angry, told him to go and jump in the lake —any lake! Sergeant York went home, all right, but the scorn of the world followed him there and made most of the rest of his life a painful experience. But, fortunately, he had a wife named Gracie, and her love was bigger and

121

stronger and tougher than all the hurt the world could throw at them.

It's hard to imagine Saul of Tarsus as a man who knew how it felt to be hurt—certainly he couldn't have persecuted the early Christians with such zest if he had ever known pain. But *Paul?*—that's another story!

Paul was still Saul when he felt pain for the first time. It was somewhere along the Damascus Road when Saul encountered Jesus Christ, and the pain he felt was the agony he was causing Christ by tormenting His followers. That's right, the pain Saul experienced was not his own, but Christ's, and it must have doubled him up. It must have opened his heart, too, because he was never the same again. He became Paul, the world's first missionary to the Gentiles, the man who sought to ease the pain in the hearts of men who knew not the Master. He was to suffer a great deal for the rest of his life, but never again did he lift his hand to cause anyone else to suffer.

Pain, hurt, and disappointment are a high price to pay for the privilege of befriending our fellowmen, but we can very well afford it. As a matter of fact, we have plenty of love, care, and concern to spend every day of our lives when our supply is fed by One who is Love itself.

# 31. "What's in It for Me?"

For quite some time the high-powered executive was the great American hero. He dominated our books, our plays, our newspapers and magazines, our fashions in clothing, our hobbies in our leisure moments, and many tried to pattern their lives after his. They respected the pushy, rugged, hard-boiled people who could look out for themselves. They weren't going to ask—they would take!

But this modern version of a high-seas pirate has gone out of style, and do you know why? This man who always asked, "What's in it for me?" finally got an answer—"Nothing!" He discovered that a lifetime dedicated to nothing and no one but himself was empty and worthless, and he began to crack up under the weight of a conscience full of selfish acts.

Now there is another hero emerging on the American scene, a much gentler person and one who seems to be getting plenty of satisfaction from offering his service to others—and often with little or no pay. We are witnessing the rise of the teacher, the social worker, the Peace Corps worker, as the hero figures, and this is a refreshing change.

And what of the high-powered executive these days? What's he doing with himself? Apparently, some of them are still running in circles, even though the spotlight of our attention no longer shines to the same degree on them —but there are some interesting exceptions, fourteen of whom are conducting an important experiment in living life over again.

These fourteen men and women, ranging in age from thirty-five to sixty, are attending an experimental series of classes at Columbia University. They are part of a program called "New Careers," and their tuition is paid by a fellowship from the Ford Foundation—all of which, in itself, isn't so unusual. What makes you sit up and take notice is the fact that only highly successful executives may participate in this program, and they are studying in fields that are totally different from the ones in which they have made their mark. These people aren't has-beens or people who have cracked under the strain of a demanding job—they're men and women who have changed horses in midstream, and at considerable expense to themselves and their families. Each one of them gave up a position that paid them more than $12,000 a year and a future that guaranteed even more, but they had a reason that made it all seem worthwhile—they wanted to be of service to their fellowman. And so they are preparing themselves for new careers in fields such as hospital or library administration, education, and social work. What's more, they know they won't be well paid.

A few of these unusual students are already working part-time in their new fields. A former sales executive is now an industrial-arts teacher in a school for deaf children; a former interior decorator now helps undereducated and underprivileged people to find the kinds of jobs they can handle; a former advertising copywriter is now a reference librarian helping students and researchers to find the books they need for their projects.

What do these people get out of this sudden switch in their lives? Do you suppose they ever ask themselves, "What's in it for me?" And what about their families?—

how must they feel about it? After all, these men and women don't have to worry about paying their tuition, but they must still go on living. Most of them are attending school full-time and can't hold part-time jobs which might offer a little financial assistance, and so they have to nibble away at their savings, at those great hoards they accumulated at such cost to themselves.

These men and women—and their families—evidently have had enough of the material forms of security and reward. They know what money can do when it takes over the driver's seat in life, and they feel pretty fortunate to be able to turn their backs on it. They want more than money out of life, and they know now that they stand a chance of getting it.

How many of us would dare to make such a change? And yet, haven't we all wished—at some time in our lives —that we could live our lives over again in order to make some improvements? What do we do when people come to us in their time of need? Do we scratch our chins and mutter, "What's in it for me?"

What's in *life* for us? Absolutely nothing, unless we're willing to roll up our sleeves and get to work helping people. Many top businessmen have discovered the thrill of combining the roles—success *and* people. That's what we were meant to do, designed by our Creator to do, and whenever we run from our total career, we're bound to end up with an empty heart, an empty life, and a full conscience to haunt our dreams.

Eventually the world will realize that it has only one Hero, one Man who sketched the only pattern of life that is fit for human beings. Isn't it a good thing Jesus Christ never asked, "What's in it for Me?"

## 32.  One Makes a Difference

How much do you suppose we're worth? I'm not talking about our value in terms of dollars and cents, but in terms of the impact each of us makes upon the world, and this is where most of us sell ourselves short. We usually don't think we count.

Well, we do count, quite a lot, especially when we put our shoulders together and tackle something big. Did you ever realize how many individual people take part in such things as a United Fund, a Community Chest, or whatever labels these fund-raising programs carry? The answer would run in the thousands, and perhaps the hundreds of thousands, and this is what enables these programs to help so many other hundreds of thousands.

Of course, if any of you have served on a committee, you know that success is not necessarily assured simply because people get together. As author Shepherd Mead said in his popular book, *How to Succeed in Business Without Really Trying*, the trouble with committees is that they usually knock the corners off an idea—and when the corners are knocked off an idea, all you have left is a blob.

If I on occasion have a little time on my hands, I sometimes spend it by walking through a park—if I can find one. Now, almost every park has its monument, and I must have gazed upon hundreds of them all over the country, but I have yet to see a monument dedicated to a committee. There are all kinds of statuary commemorating individual human beings, but nobody seems to remember a committee that did something noteworthy. That's unfair, because we all know of groups that have made great contributions to the world, but I suppose they are very few compared to the ones who simply talk themselves into a state of paralysis.

This may be a very crowded planet, but if you think that you, as an individual, don't count for much, think again! History was often made by lone human beings, and it's being made in the same old way today. This is as true in the church as it is in the business world, or anywhere else, and if you're blaming the church for getting bogged down in too many committees, then give it credit for sending some mighty individuals out into the world, too. These are the laymen who are reaching out toward the vast number of people who have left the church, for one reason or another, and they're doing a wonderful job in their quiet, solitary way. You'll find them organizing informal Bible study groups in homes, lifting up the trampled in the slums, showing society's unwanted children that someone still has faith in them.

I recently talked with a man who had had a long career in television, a man who poured most of his interest into his work and very little else. For most of his life, he had had no feeling whatever for religion of any kind, although, as he told me, he used to wonder "what people saw in it." It was too organized for him, too much a world unto itself, and, I suspect, it spoke a language he didn't understand. Then, one day, he met a Christian who didn't behave the way he thought Christians usually did—this man was warm, friendly, and completely interested in everything my friend had to say. In fact, my friend began to talk as he had never talked in his life, and

127

before he knew it he was pouring out all the loneliness, the helplessness, the fear and anxiety that any man feels when he hasn't met Christ. My friend surprised himself, but not this Christian, for he had heard these things before, many times. You see, he was a minister of a small church in Manhattan and on his days off he tried to serve as much of the rest of mankind as he possibly could. He walked the streets of New York, from one end of town to the other, concentrating most of his time in such places as Greenwich Village and the Bowery, where men and women no longer bothered to hide their lostness. He talked to people—to anyone who seemed to need a friend—and he listened to them as they broke down and told him of their misery, and he gave them hope by bringing God out of the church and into their hearts. He did the same thing for my friend.

You can meet the lost on any street, run-down or fashionable, and you don't always need a committee to go out and help them. What you can do as one person may not be much, but it may be enough to inspire others to finish the job.

I once watched a great football team that was doing very badly because their best player had to sit it out on the bench. He had injured his neck in another game a few weeks earlier, and his doctors wanted to be sure that he was completely healed before he got back into rough action, but the agony of watching his teammates groping their way around the field was worse than any physical pain he had ever felt. Finally, he could take it no longer and he began warming up to go in. His coach didn't like the prospect of losing the ball game, but he wasn't going to risk the safety of his best player, so he firmly objected when he saw what was on the young man's mind. He did not give in, even when he saw that his refusal might cause another kind of injury—to his spirit.

One man came off the field, and before a substitute player was sent in, the injured player left the bench. When the team saw who it was they could hardly keep from jumping up into the air. The spectators could see right away that there was more spring in their steps. Even under all that padding, it was evident that their shoulders were squared again.

Everyone took formation; then came the kickoff to the opposing team, and our determined player ran downfield but straight past the goalpost, through the end zone, and back to the bench! A teammate had tackled the ball carrier. They were back in winning form, thanks not least to one man who did more than his share.

I knew that player and when I talked to him shortly after the game I learned, to my surprise, that he didn't expect to do anything spectacular at all after he joined his teammates on the playing field. He just wanted to be out there with them. "What in the world would you have done if the ball carrier from the other team had come straight at you?" I asked him, and immediately I could see that such a thing hadn't entered his mind. He grinned and said, "I guess I would have jumped up as high as I could, stuck my feet out, and hoped that something good would happen."

Whatever each of us does—or doesn't do—counts. That's why caring isn't enough—unless it leads to doing. While it's true that committees often get all tangled up in themselves, some things do have to be done by a group and not by an individual. But let's not forget that a group isn't worth a thing unless each individual is doing his own thinking and making his own contribution.

If you're on a committee that isn't getting anywhere,

don't sit back and shake your head at "people" in general
—you're a part of the failure because you're a part of the
committee. And the same is true of life—you're a part of
the world's predicament because you're a part of hu-
manity.

## 33.  Never Too Many Hands

Some of us have a reason to be bitter about life. We feel we've given so much of ourselves to good causes, only to see them fail, one after another. We'd like to go on giving, but we can't help wanting to see a few results from our efforts, and so far we haven't. Has the world become a better place because we've lived in it? Have we been able to change anyone's life for the better? Have we even been a good influence on our own families? The honest answer to all these questions often turns out to be "no"—at least, as far as we can see.

But that's our trouble—we can't see very far at all, and we often miss the most important part of the scenery because we're looking for something that doesn't belong there.

The world is improved and people are changed slowly, very slowly, and hardly ever by one single person or event. Our lives are so intricately interwoven that it's literally impossible for us to see the immediate results of our actions, either good or bad—but they really don't go unnoticed. Sooner or later, the things we give to people show up in their lives, but we usually don't recognize them because they are mingled with all the other contributions made by many other people.

Not long ago, some officials in a London art gallery learned how important it was for even one person to care. They had been notified by a fifteen-year-old schoolgirl that one of their Van Gogh paintings was improperly

131

hung on the wall, and at first they dismissed her comments as absurd. Really, they thought, hundreds of people had passed by the painting, and no one had said anything about it! Then they finally took a look at the painting and found that, indeed, the young girl was absolutely correct! Van Gogh's "Grass and Butterflies" was upside down! It had been taken down for cleaning, and the workmen who replaced it obviously didn't have an eye for art. Neither did many of the gallery's visitors, it seems!

Now, I suppose we could give that little girl all the credit for detecting the error, but actually she deserves only *most* of it. Some of it belongs to those who encouraged her interest in art and possibly taught her all they knew about it—perhaps her parents and her teacher. In fact, that painting in a sense was righted by a long line of people who gave of themselves to her life, and maybe never saw the actual results of their giving.

There's a little coffee shop in Washington, D. C., where people can get the kind of care that may count for something later in their lives. It's just a tiny place, but very cozy and warm, and anybody can simply come in, sit down, have a cup of coffee, and listen to the soft background music. It's a good place to talk about whatever ails you—because the shop was established and staffed by members of a very small congregation who don't really expect to see the immediate results of the love they want to give to the world. They just want to give it—and let their love fall where it may! Over in a corner you can usually find their minister talking to someone who may be near the breaking point—perhaps someone with a drinking problem, or someone who doesn't think life is worth living any more—and you'd be amazed to see how much good a little love, a little interest, a little concern can do! This little coffee shop doesn't have any statistics about the number of lives they have saved or the number of people who have gone out with a lighter step, but they know that they're getting somewhere because their shop is becoming more crowded every day.

I always like to attend graduation ceremonies because that's where I can really see the results of a whole lot of love! A few months ago, I attended one that I'll never forget—it was in Indio, California, and the ceremonies were held outdoors in the early evening, under a clear and star-brightened sky. It was a large school, and 220 youngsters were to receive their diplomas, and were their parents proud! Yet, they had every right to be, because they had a big stake in those young people. They had put their hopes and dreams and past and future into those kids—as well as their guidance, their money, their time, and plenty of worry. Now they were getting something—something very wonderful—they were sharing in this proudest of all moments, and they knew they had a right to share!

At the very end of the list was a name that was out of alphabetical order, and for a very practical reason. The school authorities wanted to be sure that the aisles of the stadium wouldn't be filled with people when this young man came down front to get his diploma. When his name was called, people began applauding immediately, and I knew this lad must be someone very special, so I craned my neck toward the back rows, where I could hear a little commotion. I certainly wasn't prepared for the windmill of arms and legs that seemed to tumble down the aisle, and I found myself joining in the thunderous applause as hard as I could. This young man was a cerebral-palsy victim whose every move was a desperate struggle to coordinate the parts of his body—and yet he had managed to go through high school and get good

133

grades, too. In spite of all his handicaps, he was a cheerful boy, and it was easy to see why he was such a favorite with the other students. As he approached the front, his mortarboard went flying off his convulsively jerking head, but immediately hands reached out to pick it up and put it back on his head—and with such gentleness! Then, when the proud, beaming young man began his long, staggering, loose-jointed, stumbling way back, I wondered how many people (his parents and others who had reached out to him over the years) had realized that their encouragement had been so important?

All our youngsters need as much as we can give them, and some are called upon to give more than they realize they have. I know two such parents who have taught me that love can be inexhaustible. I had known them for some time before their first son was born, yet I could do so little either as pastor or friend when their doctor told them that their newborn boy was seriously malformed. There wasn't a single properly-formed bone in either of his legs, or arms, his hands were tangled masses of skin, he had a cleft palate, and the protrusions at the ends of his legs looked more like fins than feet. If ever a baby needed all the love and care in the world, it was little Tommy! And he got a lot of love from so many people, who came to care a great deal about him—but I don't suppose any one of them really thought anything would come of it. His parents were wonderful—Tommy's handicaps were a stunning blow to them, but they accepted it, and that's how they won half the battle right away. They took Tommy to the best doctors they could find, and every one of those men and women—plus many, many people on the hospital staffs—did everything they could to help the boy. Finally, sixteen years and fifty-two operations later, Tommy can say that he's doing pretty well in life. Many of his bone deformities have been surgically corrected; he also wears a pair of artificial feet which enable him to walk, run, and even ride a bicycle —and he's a very good wrestler!

If this boy ever wanted to turn around and thank all the people who made it possible for him to live a full and interesting life, he wouldn't be able to do it. There would be too many of them—and some of them would be people he has never seen. And so he thanks God, who alone makes it possible for human beings to love like that— and Tommy knows what a miracle this is! And Tommy's courage? That is a miracle too.

## 34. Walk Like a Turtle

A few months ago a friend of mine retired from an outstanding business career, and we celebrated it by getting together for a long talk. We used to have a good many of these talks years ago, when both of us seemed to have more time.

As we were reliving the "old days," my friend chuckled and reminded me of a time when he was considering changing his job. He had been with one company for several years, but he had gone as high as he could go and there was a lot more ambition left in him. What was he to do? Things were nice and secure where he was, but he was constantly bothered by a nagging little voice that kept telling him to look around the world a bit more.

I remembered the incident, and I laughed, too, for it was the beginning of a fascinating success story. You see, my friend finally mustered all his courage and simply resigned from his nice, warm, secure job and went out looking for something better. And he found it! He found a job with a company that had plenty of room for a bright, hard-working, ambitious man, and up, up he went to become comptroller of the firm.

"You know, Rube," he said, "I must have been a regular Rip Van Winkle during those early days—I was asleep for too long, and all of a sudden I woke up!"

Lots of people are great sleepers for a good part of their lives—but watch their smoke when they wake up! Grandma Moses certainly didn't waste any time when she took up her paintbrush in her old age, and she left the world so much more beautiful for the few years she lived in it as an artist.

Probably many of us are sleeping at this very minute, and we aren't even aware of it—we're sleeping because we don't realize the wonderful things we could do if only we tried. We all have talent and ability, but many of us haven't even begun to tap these resources because we don't know they exist. We haven't gotten to know ourselves, and in our ignorance we underestimate our strength, our courage, our remarkable potential.

What do we usually do when we're faced with a particularly tough job that simply has to be done? Some of us seem to thrive on difficult things in life and we rip right into them without a moment's hesitation. But some of us—the majority of people—begin to look around for a way out, and if we can't find one, we try to mark time by shifting from one foot to the other.

That's not what J. Edgar Hoover did when he was offered a job as head of the Federal Bureau of Investigation back in 1924. The F.B.I. was a very small, disorganized group of men in those days, and no one would have blamed Hoover for wanting no part of it. Why, bringing efficiency to the department and giving its men some spirit and morale seemed like an impossible task—but not to J. Edgar Hoover, who was willing *to try!* I think we'll all have to agree that he succeeded very well!

Not all of us have to reorganize governmental departments or take up painting, but many of us could do so much more than we do. We don't think much of our abilities, and perhaps this is one reason why we're so reluctant to admit that we *do* care—*deeply*—about where this world is going. I don't think *any* of us wants to go on walking a road that has never felt the tread **of**

Jesus Christ. I don't think *any* of us wants to feel his heart shriveling up inside him because he won't give a hand to a stranger, or a bit of first aid to a fallen friend, or even a trace of real love to his child. But we're all so timid, we're all so unsure of ourselves, that we're afraid to take on anything as big as caring. We just don't seem to think we're up to it!

We all could learn something from a creature as modest as a turtle. Have you ever taken the time to watch one move around? And have you ever noticed that when a turtle wants to go somewhere, to move ahead, he sticks his neck out? That's right! He can't go anywhere as long as he pulls his head and feet into his shell—and he's also quite safe there, for the time being. Why, you could knock on that shell all day long, and you'd never get a glimpse of the creature living inside. But let that turtle make up his mind to go somewhere, and out come the head and feet!

We human beings have to face the fact that we'll have to stick our necks out, too, and we may get hurt doing it. That's part of life, part of the risk of loving. We can't go on pretending that the tough jobs don't exist—they certainly do, and they're getting tougher every day. There is work for us to do in our homes, our churches, our schools, our communities, our nation, our world—and the work isn't easy. It can't be done quickly, either, and here again the turtle is a good teacher.

I guess we all remember that fable about the hare and the turtle who began a race which the hare seemed certain to win—but he didn't! The hare was overconfident and stopped for a rest along the way, and while he was sleeping, the turtle—slowly and surely as ever—passed him and went on to win the race. Now, most people take their lesson from the fact that the hare was careless, but

I can see something else in the story—I think it's quite amazing that the turtle entered the race in the first place! I think it's just great that he didn't say to himself, as we so often do, "Why, I could never beat that guy! I could never win a race with anyone!"

Why don't we stick our necks out and and get moving! Everybody is running so fast these days, and getting so lost in the tangle of their frenzied lives, that maybe we could get much farther by a slow, measured step. Besides, we're taking on an enormous assignment—we're going to get involved with life, we're going to open up our hearts, and that may be a painful experience. We certainly don't have to hurry—we must take all the time we need to be loving.

## 35.    If God Could Care—

One evening after a Board of Education meeting, it was quite obvious that one member was getting the cold shoulder from the others as they all came out of the Town Hall. Most of the men were angry because it was so late, and they had to go to work early in the morning—and the meeting wouldn't have lasted so long if it hadn't been for Joe and his silly questions! The items on the agenda had been handled efficiently, without any fuss, and the meeting was about to end when Joe began questioning some of the points that had been brought out in the discussion period. This led to some pretty long arguments, pro and con, and some of the men thought they would never get home!

Nobody said "good-night" to Joe, and then a strange thing happened. As the men were walking toward their homes, in small groups or in pairs, they began to realize that they were wrong to be so angry. Why, when they really thought about it, Joe's questions were very intelligent and they led to some interesting answers—more than one man found good reasons to change their minds about the way they were going to vote.

"I vote that we give Joe an apology," said one man. "He may hold things up a little, now and then, but you can't say he isn't interested in the school system—and he can think for himself!"

Some people never think for themselves, and as if that isn't bad enough, they don't like anybody else to do it, either. They'd like everybody to let somebody do all the thinking for all of us—and of course it would save a lot of time, wouldn't it? But I know a man who believes that thinking is worth all the time it takes—he's Thomas J. Watson, Jr., Chairman of the Board of I.B.M., a company that manufactures machines to save people time! When he was addressing some college students he said, "It's an uncommon man today who does very much real thinking for himself." I think most of us would agree with him.

It's hard to do your own thinking these days. People may make fun of you and call you a "fool," and nobody wants to go through life with that kind of a label. What a shame it is that we've lost our taste for trying something different! That's what a person is when he thinks for himself—different! He isn't a fool, and he isn't a pest, and he isn't trying to make the rest of us miserable—although he may at times succeed in doing that. But he simply may not want to accept ready-made decisions because he's quite capable of making up his own mind.

If we're really serious about wanting to get in touch with other lives, what are we going to do when we run into one of these independent characters who likes to think for himself? Is he included in our list of "fellowmen," or weren't we thinking about his kind when we said we wanted to help people? Did we intend to help those people who are just like us, and let the others be helped by their own kind—whoever they may be?

Caring doesn't mean a thing if it's done selectively. What good are our best intentions if they don't apply equally to people who "get our backs up" as well as to those who are "right down our alley"? Wasn't it this very selectivity that made some of us stop caring in the first place? Didn't we begin by saying some people weren't

141

worth our care? Now, that may not be a part of ourselves that we especially want to face, but we'd better not avoid it much longer, or it will take over the rest of our lives!

When you get right down to the issue, who are we to pick and choose among God's creatures? Sometimes we forget who our relatives are and we behave as if God made only *some* of us—which is one of the worst lapses of memory a man can have! It means that he begins to think that Jesus Christ suffered and died and rose again for only a handful of us, and that just makes a mockery of the cross itself.

That was a tremendous sacrifice Christ made on Calvary, and He certainly didn't make it just for a group of His closest friends. If ever a man talked to people straight-from-the-shoulder, it was the Son of God, and He put His own disciples in their place when they got some of the same foolish notions we sometimes get today. ". . . They that be whole need not a physician, but they that are sick" (MATTHEW 9:12, KJV), He told them, and His words were meant for us, too.

We all want to "be ourselves" these days, and that's fine—as long as we don't object when other people are "themselves," too. God wants us to be ourselves, the selves He created; He wants each of us to realize that we were not poured into a mold that set the pattern for millions of other people exactly like us. Each one of us is distinct, an original, and that is a mark of God's great love for us —He created each of us with special care, and for that reason alone we ought to have respect for ourselves. This is very important, because we can't really respect others, and their differences from us, until we respect ourselves and our own individuality.

". . . Let no man despise thee" (TITUS 2:15, KJV), Paul said, and we should take his advice seriously. You may live in a house just like your neighbor's, and a hundred other neighbors—you may see hundreds of automobiles just like yours, your children may dress and talk like all the other children on the block, and some people may even tell you that you look like someone else—but you're still one in a million, or a billion, or a trillion, or however many people inhabit this earth! *Nobody* is just like you—not even your own children!—and this is true of each and every other human being.

We are all valued children of God, and maybe one of these days we'll look upon each other as He does. Somehow He manages to go on loving each of us—in spite of our differences with Him, our stubbornness in trying to go our own way in life, and our constant bickering with each other. When we can begin to care in such a way as He does, we will realize that there is no such thing as an unimportant person, or an unworthy person, and when our lives touch the lives of others—with warmth and compassion—we will each know the magnificent sense of glory that is given to every true servant of God.

## 36.  No One Else Will Know

What a terrible time some of us have trying to master the fine art of keeping our big mouths shut! How very few people can be entrusted with something confidential when they know the world would just love to hear about it! Keeping our trust with others often demands a kind of bigness many of us don't seem to have—it takes a kind of spirit most of us haven't yet caught from Jesus Christ.

I suppose we're inclined to accept our little weakness as part of our way of life, but it's really very serious. It cuts us off from each other at the point where we may need each other most.

Did you ever realize how fortunate you are to be able to sit down and talk to someone you know? Many people wouldn't dare, because they know they might just as well sit down and talk to a microphone hooked up to the four corners of the world! This is especially true of people in highly responsible positions. They desperately need to unburden themselves to another human being who can understand their problems, but they hardly ever do. Oh, maybe they tried it a few times, when they didn't know any better—maybe they talked to their boss, or a business associate, or a close friend, and then they made the pain-ful, embarrassing discovery that they simply couldn't trust that other person to keep his mouth shut. The man just wasn't big enough to hold onto his share of a confidence. And for this reason, many heavily burdened people are torn apart on the inside. They burn, they struggle, they wrestle with their immense decisions—completely alone and often convinced that nobody really cares about them.

I don't think we mean to be disloyal or untrustworthy when we break a confidence for the sake of gossip, but that's what we are. If the description fits us too well, perhaps we haven't taken a good look at ourselves recently. We're going on and on about other people and the lives they lead, but what about us and the lives we live? Isn't that a matter for our intense care and concern, too?

Before we get back in touch with the world, how about getting in touch with ourselves? How about this thing called "integrity"? What kind of shape is ours in?

Integrity isn't easy to find—it's far down in our souls, and it has a lot to do with the way we feel there. It isn't something we can use to impress the world, because it's something no one else—except God—can see. But when a person has it, somehow we can sense it, although not always immediately.

The late Herbert Hoover had integrity, but the world didn't become aware of it until near the end of his long lifetime. For years that man endured the most humiliating jokes, the most abusive assaults on his character and intelligence, and some downright cruel expressions of hatred—yet he never fought back, even when he was blamed for things he hadn't done. Herbert Hoover went on living as he had always lived—with dignity, poise, gentleness, humility, and great integrity. Perhaps he was uncomfortable among the people of his time, but down deep in his soul he was serene. Sometimes, if a man lives long enough, he is justified in the eyes of the world, and Americans rejoiced when this happened to Herbert Hoover. In the later years of his life he was recognized as a truly outstanding leader, a man who could not only remain silent when he was falsely accused, but a man who could also come through a difficult time with his soul untouched by bitterness. I think this teaches us that the little things in our character matter a great deal. They make up the separate, individual, little vertebra in the backbone of our integrity.

Before we try to help a brother, we ought to find out whether we can be of any real help to him—or to anyone. We can spend the rest of our lives ministering to the needs of others without ever giving them something meaningful—unless we ourselves have found a meaning in our own lives.

This lack of meaning is one of the greatest woes in life today, and you can see it staring out of the eyes of a multimillionaire as well as those of a poverty-stricken child. It tells us that our physical lives just aren't enough to satisfy us.

No man can find meaning in life unless everything he does is related to his faith. He must know the love of God as a personal experience before he can share it with another human being; he must *feel* the healing touch of the forgiveness that was made possible through the death of Christ before he can forgive another who may have hurt him; he must realize that he was created to know yet another life, a life eternal in the presence of the Eternal, before he can cherish the eternal values in another's soul.

Such a man finds his rest in God, and he is undisturbed by all the clamor in this world. He hears one thing—the voice of God—and this is what directs him and gives his life power and meaning. He feels completely at home in his soul, and he doesn't worry if no one else knows it— as long as God does.

## 37.  Get Lost!

How do we really know when people are troubled?
They don't always tell us and some of them are very
good at covering up. How do we know when they need
us?

Jesus can give us an answer to these questions, because
if ever anyone heard the cries that no one else could hear,
it was He. None of us, for instance, might have noticed
that nasty little tax collector sitting up in a tree as Jesus
passed by—and if we had happened to notice him, we
certainly wouldn't have dreamed that anything could
bother him! Not that one! Why, he reduced whole
families to starvation by overtaxing them—and then he
kept most of all he collected. It took a lot of money to pay
for that fancy house he owned, and everybody knew that
he threw lavish parties almost every night!

No, if we were to judge by outer signs, we couldn't
have believed that Zacchaeus needed anyone's sympathy
—but Jesus had another way of looking at a human being.
He looked into their souls and that's where He found
the misery we so often miss. He saw Zacchaeus up in the
tree—high above the heads of the other people who were
craning their necks for a look at the Master as He passed
by on His donkey—and He saw a totally desolate man, a
man whose heart cried out for just a little kindness. And
instead of telling Himself that Zacchaeus didn't know the
meaning of kindness when other people begged him for
it, Jesus gave him kindness without limit.

But how did Jesus know that Zacchaeus needed it? Did he detect men's yearnings by divine means, or did He set an example that we can follow?

Aren't we forgetting something? What do we think Jesus was doing here on earth? Wasn't He putting Himself in man's shoes during those thirty-three years He walked the earth? Doesn't He know exactly how we all feel simply because He has lived our lives?

Jesus had a sensitivity that no one will ever be able to match, but we are not without a healthy trace of it in our own beings. While Jesus could understand all of us in all our human situations, we should be able to understand at least some of us. But if we look only at the surface of other lives, we will learn nothing about them. Certainly a man like Zacchaeus could have troubles—big troubles! —but we can hardly understand what they might have been until we imagine how we might feel if we lived as he did.

How would we feel if we loved money so much that we squeezed it out of everybody—rich and poor alike—in the name of doing our job? How would we sleep at night after a day of turning away from the cries of the poor, who had to go without their stale crust of daily bread so that we might add one more penny to our growing hoard? What would we do when we were alone and could safely give way to our tears of anguish and shame over our inability to be kind, to be generous, to be merciful? Would we really enjoy the company of other people? Wouldn't we feel twice as lonely at our big parties because we realized that people attended them only to get a free meal?

If we let ourselves be guided by Jesus Christ, we're going to find much more suffering than we ever knew existed. We're going to walk through hearts and souls that writhe in pain—and we're going to feel some of it right along with them. But that's the only way to discover where we're needed. We have to become completely sensitive to all other people, not just those who are most like us, and we have to be prepared for some surprises.

We're going to find that, in spite of our individual personality differences, we are all pretty much the same. We share some of the same burdens, the same struggles, the same perplexities, the same fears, the same temptations—and in that sense we all belong to each other. Other people aren't a pile of bricks—they're flesh-and-blood, just as you are, as I am—and they are molded by the way you and I treat them.

If we can allow ourselves to give of ourselves as soon as we sense a need, we may have some of the same results that Jesus had with people. Zacchaeus, for instance, certainly didn't know what kindness meant, even though his heart must have longed for it, but perhaps he had never been given any kindness until he met Jesus. Once he knew what kindness meant, he was able—even eager—to give it to others, and this accounts for the amazing change that took place in his life. It really wasn't so strange that a man with his past would want to give away so much of his worldly goods. He had discovered the true joy in life—the joy of losing oneself in giving oneself!

This is a joy we too can experience, but first we have to lose ourselves in the lives and feelings of other people. Then, when we no longer need to be told what it is they need so badly, we'll know exactly what to do.

## 38. A Touch of Warmth

Wouldn't we all polish up our manners if we realized that a little courtesy could save our lives? Well, it can, at least when we're driving a car.

Did you know that a great many of our worst automobile accidents are caused by a complete lapse of courtesy when some people get behind the wheel of a car? I really can't explain what happens, but many a man who wouldn't dream of preceding a lady through an open door will often cut off a driver who has the right of way at an intersection. And how many of us try to get away from a light ahead of the others cars, or pass another car on the right because the driver is too slow for our tastes? And haven't we all honked our horns because a driver in front of us didn't take off as soon as the light turned green?

The absence of good manners on the road can be illustrated very dramatically with statistics on the number of accidents it causes, but the lack of courtesy in everyday habits of living is a little harder to spot. But it's there—it shows up in a general attitude of coldness among people, a coldness that forces them farther and farther apart from each other, and this is an area where much of our care is needed.

Our modern world needs warmth, lots of it. I don't mean the central-heating kind of warmth, because we have plenty of that in every conceivable form—I mean the kind of warmth that can be felt when people are just plain nice to each other.

An elderly character-actor died recently, and although he wasn't the big star he used to be many years ago, he had top billing along the streets he walked on his way to and from his home in Hollywood. It always took him a long time to get anywhere because he never passed anyone by with only a nod. He would always stop to say a few words to his friends and neighbors, to ask how they felt and how the rest of their family were doing.

Now he's gone, and we can understand why his friends miss him very much. I've often thought about people like him—people who make a difference to other people, people who warm up the lives of others—and I think they are the real success stories in modern life.

Victor Borge once said something that describes another kind of experience—the kind most of us have with people. He said, "Why is it that I can't get dark spots when I wear a dark suit, and light spots when I wear a light suit? I always get the dark spots on the light suit, and the light spots on the dark suit!" That's the story of us and our relationship with others! We mean well and behave badly. But does it have to be that way?

I wonder if we can't try to live with a little warmth for people, a little patience and understanding for the times when they might not be sitting on top of the world. Do we always have to snap back when somebody snaps at us? Couldn't we possibly ask if we can be of any help?

Quite possibly we could prevent a lot of the irritation that builds up in people if we tried to express some appreciation for a job well done. It doesn't have to be a big job—any job done well deserves a "thank-you" note. If you've ever received one, you know how much it means.

I always used to plan to write notes of appreciation, but I seldom got around to them. They always seemed to require so much time that I needed for other things. Occasionally, if I had the opportunity, I'd say a word of thanks in passing, and I guess that means more than nothing—but not very often a note. One day I was put to shame by a friend of mine who was sitting next to me on a plane.

I've seen a lot of plane landings over the years, but never one as smooth as that one! The big plane touched ground with all the grace of a large-winged bird, which was a credit to the pilot. It just happened, too, that my friend was an official of the airline that owned the plane, and I couldn't help thinking that the pilot had certainly picked the right time to execute a perfect landing. But that wasn't the way my friend thought. "Well, I guess that pilot deserves a word of thanks," he said, and right then and there he scribbled out a note and gave it to the stewardess. Then he wrote another to the pilot's boss and told him what a fine pilot he had. I think it took him all of five minutes to write those notes, and he wasn't even late getting off the plane!

Warming the lives of others as we go our daily way is part of the Christian experience—because we receive warmth from the Christ who loves us, understands us, saves us. We have no business being cold toward each other, because we live with such hope in our hearts. Why, we can afford to say "Thank you" to many every day of the year!

152

## 39. Give a Soul a Break

As long as we're warming up to the rest of the world, why don't we take a giant step forward and give some soul a break? Lots of souls could use one.

Not everyone can keep up with the frantic pace of today's life, and some of us fall behind. We have to take time out, so to speak, to repair the damage we do to ourselves, but while we are recuperating, the world rushes on by and we stand very little chance of ever catching up with it.

A few years ago, a governor of a southeastern state finished his final term of office and went from the governor's mansion straight down to the gutter. He had been such a promising young man, a real political "comer," and he became filled with the anticipation of success. Nothing could seem to stop him, and so he became careless. He celebrated a little too much, then a little too early, then all the time—just he and a bottle, and before long he couldn't put that bottle down. He managed to finish his term in office by fighting off his habit as hard as he could during working hours, but when his job was done he pulled out all the stops. It was Skid Row—the end of family, career, self-respect, and the beginning of endless misery.

Then, quite recently, this man was recognized by a reporter, who happened to hail his cab one day in Chicago. It was amazing that the reporter was able to make the connection between the youthful, robust, visibly competent man who had once looked so right on his way up the capitol steps, and the tired, aged, struggle-lined cab driver, and it was only natural for him to want to know what had happened over the years. And so they talked—the reporter and man who had been forgotten—and a very interesting story came out. The former governor had hit bottom, all right, but he hadn't stayed there. Something in him simply had to start fighting again, and he began his slow, painful climb up out of the gutter. It wasn't a steady climb; he fell back many times, but finally he made it, and he hoped he wouldn't fall back again. Then, and only then, he got in touch with his family. When the reporter found him, he was holding down a steady job, seeing his family on weekends, and gradually readjusting to a life he dared to call "normal."

"What do you think?" asked the reporter, somewhat hesitantly, "Can you ever be a lawyer again? I mean, can you make a real comeback?"

The taxi driver met his passenger's eyes in the mirror. "I think maybe I'm ready," he said softly, "but I'm not sure that the world is."

Perhaps that man, who has since died of cancer, knew the rest of us as well as he knew himself. We aren't always ready to welcome back the ones who fall behind. Oh, yes, we cheer them on and tell them to straighten their backbones and stiffen their upper lips, but we usually close ranks as soon as they drop out of our lives. Then, when they want to come back in, there's no room for them.

Most of us are becoming alarmed by statistics on the increasing number of school dropouts and students who just can't seem to keep up with their class. Nobody seems to know what to do about this problem, although all sorts of experts have studied it.

But in one Long Island community, the people decided that they needed a very special kind of expert if their emotionally disturbed youngsters were ever going to get any real help. They needed something called "teacher-moms," and out of an entire town they got exactly twelve of them—twelve housewives who were willing to spend a few hours a week teaching a slow or troubled child in their own homes. There was only one qualification for this job—and it had nothing to do with a degree, because only a few of these women had any experience as teachers, and one or two hadn't even graduated from high school—and that was a basic capacity to love a child. Apparently it was a very rare quality, but it certainly worked wonders.

Twelve housewives took twelve youngsters under their wings and they taught them so much more than their readin', writin', and 'rithmetic. They taught those kids that people *did* care about them, that they *could* take time out from their mad race and explain something clearly—over and over, if necessary—because they wanted them to understand the world around them. The results weren't evident overnight, but after a while everyone could see that those kids began to take a vital interest in their studies. They wanted to take their places in the world, because they believed there was some room for them, after all.

We can't simply cheer people on and give them our best wishes. We have to make room for them in our own lives. We have to give them as much care as they need, without any hope of getting something back. If we don't, we won't really be able to keep them out of our lives, because they'll force their way in when they become angry enough.

I imagine everyone can remember running into a bully somewhere in his childhood. There was always at least one, and what pleasure he used to take in making us shake with fear! You could hardly believe that such a boy —or girl—ever needed a break, and yet he must have needed one very badly at one time, and somebody must have said "no." It's one of life's strangest puzzles, but some of today's hardest characters were yesterday's biggest softies.

There are lots of softies in the slums today, but I hate to think of the kind of people they'll become unless the world makes a little more room for them. Sometimes a bit of space is all they need, and perhaps some peace and quiet. At least, that's what is being offered to some city boys by a very fashionable private school in Connecticut. Some time ago, the officials of Hotchkiss School decided to offer their facilities to city boys during the summer months when the school otherwise would have been vacant. They wanted to find out whether underprivileged boys could really get any benefit from a more comfortable way of life; they wanted to find out whether there was any point in trying to help these boys at all. Well, the results were beyond belief. Not only did the boys become as quiet and peaceful as the sloping hills around the school, but they took an intense interest in their classes. In fact, the project offered so much encouragement that the school officials decided to continue it for at least three more summers.

The world may be getting pretty crowded, but there is still plenty of room in the human heart. That's one place that should never carry a "No Vacancy" sign on it—and if Jesus Christ lives there, it never will.

## 40. Know You're Alive!

Just off a southern freeway you can see a high hill almost covered with trucks, cranes, and huge earth-movers winding their way up and down a spiraling road. It's an interesting scene, and so is the story behind it.

This funny old hill was once a sort of "sore thumb" right in the middle of some beautiful ranch land owned by a man with two sons. The hill was too big to be leveled, and so it just sat there, bald and barren, doing nothing at all. In a way it was somewhat like the man's younger son, a nice boy who couldn't seem to do anything very well. The father used to tell himself that it was a good thing he had two sons, because the older one certainly made up for the lack of promise in the younger— here was a lad with a real future!

I guess the similarities between his land and his sons must have stuck in the old man's mind, because when he died he left the better part of his land—the rich ranch land—to his older son in the hope that he would continue to increase its value. To the younger son he left that funny old hill and the surrounding property.

A very strange thing happened to that property after it passed into the next generation's hands. The older boy, while a good and willing worker, had a completely undisciplined nature and was a very poor manager of money and property. In no time at all, he began to sell off small parcels of his prized land because he just didn't have his father's head for business. Soon he had nothing left.

The younger boy, on the other hand, must have made up his mind to show the world that he could make something of his legacy. He took a look at that old hill and saw that nothing would grow on it, and so he began to dig into it—maybe he was convinced that the hill, like everything else in God's creation, was good for something. Sure enough, he found that it was full of very valuable stone—in fact, it turned out to be the most valuable piece of land on his father's entire estate! The young man also had a highly disciplined mind—just the kind the business world needs—and he used it to turn his raw material into a very profitable industry.

Probably the biggest difference between these two young men was that one made the mistake of thinking he was supposed to get something out of life, while the other simply put everything he had into life. The older boy made a mistake many of us make, and this is one of the primary reasons why we feel that life has let us down. We look upon our existence as a sort of drawing account that is given to us at our birth, and we go on taking amounts from it at various intervals until it just runs out —and in some cases it runs out at a very young age. Perhaps we're all so afraid of running out of life that we begin to hoard it, to spend it ever so frugally and only on ourselves.

How wrong we are to be so stingy! Why, the life that really counts—the life that is ours through Jesus Christ— can't possibly be used up! In fact, the more we give it away, the more it thrives! And the best way to give it away is to be loving of other people.

We have come to love a great many things in our time. We love ideals, progress, intelligence, education, art, civilization, freedom, fairness, loyalty, decency—just about everything except *people*. We still have a hard time loving *them*! Yet this is what our Lord wants us to do.

Oh, it's easy to love so many other things! We can curl up in our corners, read our books, think our thoughts, practice our physical skills, design our buildings—just like that! But loving people is so much harder—sometimes it seems impossible! People don't do anything to *make* us love them!

Do you suppose people were any different when Jesus walked among them? Do you think He came to earth, prepared to make such an incredible sacrifice, because people were so wonderful? They certainly weren't, and they didn't deserve one shred of the love He showed them. But that's the point—He loved them because they were *people*, because they belonged to His Father, and this is the only kind of love that will ever mean anything in this world.

We may think of our world as just an old barren hill that somebody left to us, but before we give it up, why don't we try to dig into it a little? That's the only way we'll discover its true value.

Life is a very demanding experience. It asks of us all that we have, and unless we are willing to meet that demand we will never know what it is to be alive. We have to mingle with people, just as Jesus did, and we have to feel them react to us. We have to get close enough to hear their hearts beating in our ears, to feel their laughter building up in our throats, and to feel our eyes smarting with their tears. This is the life that we were given to live!

Ours is a world full of experts—you can find them in almost any field you can name—but where are the experts in the most important subject on earth, *people*? We've all been running away from our real vocation, and it's no wonder we aren't getting something out of all our huffing and puffing.

Today, the bell is ringing in another schoolroom,

and we had better hurry before we are too late. There are no entrance examinations for this course because all of us are eligible to enter—whether we be bright or slow, rich or poor, successful or failures, best- or least-known, we are all welcome. This is the school of love and it is taught by our Lord—and our need for it is very great.

Who cares? God cares. And because He does, we can too.